Tom & Julia Davis

Tom & Julia Davis
"Some Good Place"
– Boise, Idaho –

Susan M. Stacy

T&J PUBLISHING
Boise, Idaho

T&J Publishing, 3100 Crescent Rim, Suite 408, Boise, ID 83706

Printed in the United States of America

Cataloging-in-Publication Data

Stacy, Susan M., 1943-
Tom and Julia Davis: "Some Good Place," Boise, Idaho.

x, 137 p.; 23 cm

Includes bibliographic references and index.
ISBN 978-0-9798767-1-4 (alk. paper)
1. Frontier and pioneer life—Idaho—Boise. 2. Agriculture—Idaho—Boise.
3. Idaho—Boise—History. 4. Julia Davis Park (Boise, Idaho)—History.
I. Davis, Thomas J., 1836-1908—Biography. II. Davis, Julia McCrum,
1847-1907—Biography. III. Title.

Front cover and end papers: "A Bird's Eye View of Boise, Idaho, 1890," lithograph by Augustus Koch. Used by permission of Boise State University Albertsons Library, Special Collections Department.

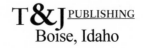

T&J PUBLISHING
Boise, Idaho

Anyone who works to make our city a good place to live is a pioneer.
This book is dedicated to you.

History is the essence of innumerable biographies.
— *Thomas Carlyle*

Contents

Introduction   ix

Prelude: An Orchard   1

One: The Sons of Mary Ann Davis   3

Two: Idaho   15

Three: Boise   23

Four: Apples   33

Five: Women   39

Six: Marion   49

Seven: Cattle   53

Eight: Leading Citizen   65

Nine: Julia Goes to the Fair   75

Ten: The Park   85

Afterword   93

Acknowledgements   97

Appendix A: Davis Family Tree   101

Appendix B: Julia Davis Park
    Selected Historical Highlights   103

Notes   109

Bibliography   125

Index   129

– Introduction –

When I first began researching the lives of Tom Davis and Julia McCrum Davis, I wondered what the theme of their story would be. Very little written by their own hands has survived: only a handwritten will and two letters. No business records, diaries, or journals. Since those things usually shed light on a person's movements, ambitions, intentions, conflicts, joys and troubles—the stuff of biography—I made a leap of faith that other materials would supply a pathway to understanding their lives.

I had certain questions to ask: where did they come from? what kind of upbringing did they have? what became of Tom's younger brother? why did they come to the Boise River valley? what did they do? what kind of partnership did Tom and Julia have? why did they give so much riverfront property to Boise City for a park?

Luckily, the couple left "tracks." Evidence of their social and business enterprises piled up from old issues of *The Idaho Statesman,* census records, the papers of the Columbian Club of Boise, and deed books. Their house was near the Boise River, where Oregon Trail travelers were likely to encounter the Davis orchard and the family that lived there. At least one of them wrote about his meeting with the Davis family in

1882—and handed me the title of this book. Because Tom was successful, his contemporaries placed short sketches of his life in their Idaho histories—always complimentary, sometimes contradictory.

Tom and Julia were Boise "pioneers," a word that headlined newspaper items about their deaths and funerals, and appeared again in their eulogies. At first, I took this word to mean merely that they were among the first to settle in the Boise River valley. But that simple fact does not explain the reverence and honor paid to pioneers by Boisean's of later generations, particularly in the 1920s and 1930s. Capitol Boulevard's bridge over the Boise River in 1931 was dedicated as a memorial to those who had traveled the Oregon Trail. The newspaper celebrated pioneers regularly in its Sunday editions. At a time when newspapers were not in the habit of covering every death and funeral in their daily pages, "pioneers" often received several inches of ink. In the 1930s, the *Statesman* sponsored the Pioneer Village in Julia Davis Park, a feature that continues today.

The evidence began to show that Tom and Julia Davis had a certain consciousness as to what they were about. Their tracks illuminated several consistent themes in their lives. Perhaps the most significant one is that they stayed in the valley and spent their life energy here. Tom acquired a modest-sized stake in a gold claim and began a process of reinvesting it over and over—here. He prospered not so much by luck as by consistent labor applied to promising ideas. Based on that one surviving letter he wrote, he appears to have been as proud of his sausage-making efforts as he must have been of his hugely productive orchard. Julia came to Boise for adventure out west, but she found a partnership worth staying for—here.

They were part of a community of people who mostly supported each others' ideas for improvement and progress. They invested in each other and in their mutual visions for an ever-better life. The revered status that cloaked Tom and Julia Davis was due to far more than being first or early in the valley. It cloaked the ones who stayed. Their story will tell us why.

AN ORCHARD

T all Tom Davis packed his saddlebags with gold dust and gold coins. He dressed his lanky frame in well-worn clothes and organized his blanket roll and other gear for a long trip. Loading his horse, he turned from Boise City toward Portland, where he was to collect a shipment of apple trees. He knew exactly what variety he wanted, and he had ordered seven thousand. He planned to pay cash at $1.25 each.[1]

Tom intended to plant the trees in 1864. He had every reason to be sure of his plan. Aside from horticultural experience in Illinois, he had experienced two winters in mining camps and knew first-hand what it was like to go for months without the pleasure of something so simple as an apple. The absence of fresh food was a fact of life in mining camps because of snow-choked passes, slow travel, and no way to preserve most products. His downstream neighbor Tom Slater had managed to plant a few fruit trees during the 1863 growing season. Evidently, they had survived. Tom Davis anticipated a very large market and laid substantially larger plans.[2]

The long trail to Umatilla was a risk; it attracted robbers, bandits, and other cheaters the likes of whom Tom Davis already knew well. To protect his gold, he gilded it with nonchalance. When stopping for the night, he threw his saddlebags carelessly to the ground and ignored them, turning

Courtesy of Ron Joyner, bighorsecreekfarm.com

Red June apple. Unlike many early ripeners, the Red June is good for fresh eating. Tom Davis took full advantage of its versatility for pie making, cider, vinegar, and drying.

his attention to whatever companions happened to be sharing the camp. No one suspected that he carried a fortune. Safe in Portland, he exchanged the gold for trees.[3]

The return trip had challenges of a different sort. The trees needed protection from whatever threats the weather and terrain had on offer: too much heat or cold, too much wet or dry. Sometimes packers paused at streams to douse botanical goods with water. Tom supervised the freighting of the trees and oversaw their safe transfer from the boat at Umatilla to the pack string headed for Boise.

On schedule in Boise, he planted the trees. Most or all of them were Red Junes, a variety suited perfectly to his vision of the market. They were highly productive and ripened early, sacrificing nothing in the way of brisk flavor for pies, cider, or eating out of hand. The trees grew straight and bore heavily, sometimes even bearing a second crop in the fall. It was just as Tom Davis had expected.[4]

— *Chapter One* —

THE SONS OF MARY ANN DAVIS

Mary Ann Davis of Cincinnati could not write her name and
owned very little. In 1830 she was a fresh young bride married
to John Davis, a woodman and carpenter. With him, she had
a chance for a better life.

The couple had their first child, Emily, in 1831. After their son, Thomas
Jefferson, was born in 1836, the family moved to Warren County, Illinois,
the western edge of the Illinois frontier. From Monmouth, its county seat,
it was only sixteen miles farther west to the Mississippi River. Mary Ann's
second son, Francis Marion, was born in Monmouth in 1838.[1]

Warren County was a promising place for a carpenter. Its landscape of
broad rolling prairie was traversed by well-wooded streams. The soil was
rich and dark, capable of supporting remarkable wealth just beneath its
tough blanket of sod. Illinois had been a state since 1818, but this western
corner, known as a "military reserve," remained unsurveyed and unsettled
until 1825, its potential resources unknown to the general populace.[2]

Illinois created counties in an orderly and rectangular fashion wherever
its geography allowed. Warren County was a perfect rectangle, its fifteen
"townships" each thirty-six square miles. Pioneer settlers had not entered
the area prior to the government's survey, a situation in striking contrast

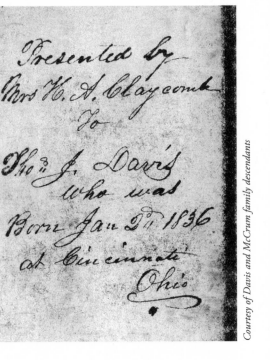

Tom Davis' Bible. Like many mothers who gave their sons a Bible to take West when they left home, Harriet Claycomb gave one to Tom. She reminded him of his birth year, 1836, but census takers, early Idaho historians, even his gravestone gave him later dates.

Courtesy of Davis and McCrum family descendants

to the squatting that took place everywhere in Idaho Territory when its sparkling resources later became known to the general populace.[3]

The first pioneers arrived in Warren County in the late spring of 1827, intent on farming. They leaned into the sod and broke it open for the first time. Despite the superb soil, there was no land rush. Two years later, all of Warren County contained only 130 families, mostly from Kentucky and eastern Illinois. The population was too small for self-government, so anyone who wished to record legal transactions had to journey fifty miles east to Peoria.

When the citizens were ready for local government they petitioned a judge in the neighboring county for the privilege. Soon, they elected three commissioners, a sheriff, and a coroner. The townships also elected legal officers known as esquires, who had the power to marry and carry out other duties, blending the tasks of justices of the peace and police.[4]

John Davis found good work in Warren County. The forested areas allowed for an architecture of log buildings. His skills began at the tree, where he selected and felled the timber he would need for barns and houses. He owned all the tools required to hew a log, shape it, and fit it for floors, walls, roofs, and doors: broad ax, adze, hatchet, whetstones, steel square, rip saw. He finished his buildings with his many specialized planes, chisels, mallets, files, compasses, augers, and hammers. His tool chest contained assorted screws, hinges, nails, and bolts.[5]

Mary Ann, together with her husband, accumulated a complimentary set of tools and goods needed to run their growing household. Mary Ann's kitchen contained a churn, a brass kettle, three metal pots, and a hand bellows. They had some carpet, a brass clock, a settee, and eight chairs. They had bed ticking and blankets, a desk and a mirror. The children had their clothes and bedding, little else. In addition to the Holy Bible, the family also owned a "school bible," a few other books and a map of the United States. They had at least one horse and saddle and a cow. John owned a silver watch, a shaving glass, and one pair of suspenders. The family had their necessities and a little more. They surely hoped to prosper.[6]

In 1839 John Davis was completing a contract to build a barn and granary for a Warren County man named Polaski Skovil. He had begun in July the year before to locate the timber in the woods. He needed good-sized trees, as the contract specified sills one foot square, and posts and beams ten inches square. He was to hew the logs in the woods and then cut and hew the rafters, floor joists, and ridgepole. This done, Skovil agreed to haul the hewn timbers to the building site, where Davis would then raise the barn 40 feet wide and 64 feet long. Skovil wanted Davis to build the interior furnishings—a granary, manger, and rack, all to provide comfortably for Skovil's horses. Altogether, the job would pay Davis $300 in three installments: $75 once he had hewed the timbers, $75 after he erected the frame, and the rest when the whole—the floors, the siding, the doors, and the roof—was finished "in a good and workmanlike manner."[7]

Skovil expected Davis to finish the job by July 4, 1839. Undoubtedly, this schedule allowed for drying the timbers for some months before erecting the barn. When the two signed their contract, John wrote his own name.

Around September 1839 John Davis died, perhaps before he finished the barn, as his contract with Skovil became part of the record when Warren County probated his estate. None of the other court documents reveal what caused his death or its precise date. Cholera visited Warren County from time to time, claiming many lives when it came. But in this sparsely settled place, wagon accidents, drowning, infection, and other diseases also were apt to take someone's life at an early age.[8]

Now Mary Ann Davis was alone. Her children were under ten years of age, Frank an infant. The couple had not owned land, and she had few resources or marketable skills. Unable to write or read, she was poorly equipped even to administer the estate of her husband. The court appointed three men to this task.[9]

Mary Ann must have been exceedingly stressed. Widows like her knew they could not easily survive alone. Another woman in western Illinois of the 1830s, Rebecca Burlend, contemplated the prospect of her husband's death after he fell upon the blade of a scythe and badly injured and infected his knee:

> *My situation requires no comment: I could not but perceive I was likely to lose my dearest earthly friend, and with him all visible means of supporting myself, or maintaining my family. I was almost driven to frenzy. Despair began to lay hold of me with his iron sinews…I saw a short time would determine whether I was to be reduced to a situation the most wretched imaginable…"*[10]

The John Davis estate administrators appraised the family's possessions even to the last detail of "one yard black muslin." John and Mary Ann had been sending Emily for schooling. They owed a fee to the teacher for the 1839 school year. The administrators paid it and collected from others what small sums they had owed to John. But in the end, Mary Ann was unable to provide for her children.

According to the practice of the day, one option was to place her children in a better situation by "binding them out." The indenturing of children was a legal means to remove a child from an "unsatisfactory" home without a long and complicated court procedure. Whether Mary Ann initiated this procedure as a way of coping with her poverty or was obliged to cooperate with the court for other "unsatisfactory" conditions is not known. Technically, parents had to agree to the indenture.

On November 26, 1840, the probate judge ordered Warren County officials, "You are hereby commanded to take the bodies of Emily Davis and Thomas J. Davis, minor heirs of John Davis deceased, if they can be found in your county, and forthwith bring them before me at my office in Monmouth..." At this place he interviewed all concerned and determined that binding them out would be the best way to promote their welfare.[11]

The court apparently sent Emily and Thomas to different households. Thomas went to the farm of Esquire Andrew and Harriet Ann Claycomb. When little Frank was old enough to leave his mother, he too was bound out to the Claycombs.

The Claycombs had been early arrivals in Warren County. Harriet Ann Whitman, a girl among twelve children, arrived in 1830, where her family settled in Cold Brook Township, east of Monmouth. Six years later, a branch of the Claycomb family arrived from Kentucky. Andrew Claycomb also took up land in Cold Brook, not far from the Whitman place. Five years later, he and Harriet Ann married.[12]

The couple remained childless. Most likely, this was a severe disappointment, for the labor of children was an asset on farms, where the endless demands of creating something out of nothing required the industry, competence, and back-breaking work of both heads of the house and all other members of the household. Birth rates on the Illinois frontier (and other American frontiers) were very high—ten or more children were common. Cash money was in short supply for most settlers, and the only way to transform the wilderness was by sheer labor.

The boys were expected to work for Claycomb in return for their support until they became adults. They had no rights and, in the eyes

Harriet Ann Whitman Claycomb (1821-1901). As a pioneer herself of the western frontier of Illinois, she raised five orphaned or indentured children, including Tom and Frank Davis.

of the law, could expect no inheritance from the Claycombs. However, by living on a farm managed by an ambitious farmer, the boys had the advantage of witnessing and helping Claycomb transform his pioneer farm into a prosperous one.

The Claycombs—and others in Warren County—were part of a wave of pioneers who went to Illinois after 1830 to better themselves and build a society to their liking. An earlier wave had gone to southern Illinois, forced out of Indiana and southern Kentucky when land ran out. The soil there, and thus opportunity, were not as rich as in the north. Historians of Illinois have said that the southern folk tended to work only hard enough to get by from one year to the next.

In the north, the pioneers settled with every intention to produce crops for as big a market as they could find or create. They did this by building roads and railroads to potential markets. They trusted modern innovations and education to improve agricultural output. They had faith in reason, possessed a drive for middle-class status and equal rights, and held a sense of mission in their powers to improve the world. They were future-oriented. They regarded gambling, wasting time, fighting, and drunkenness as evils. In assigning status to various occupations, they valued those which required education. In the ten years after 1830, the new pioneers established a dozen colleges in Illinois, despite the sparsity of the population.[13]

The Claycombs exposed Mary Ann Davis' boys to these attitudes and ideas. If Andrew Claycomb was a whole-hearted exemplar of a "modern" farmer, he would have gone to county fairs to learn about new methods, experimented with new seeds, and considered new animal breeds. He would have subscribed to *Prairie Farmer,* a forward-looking magazine. As an "esquire," Claycomb had a responsible position in the community beyond his own farm. His name frequently appeared in the *Monmouth Atlas* as the one who had married some happy couple.[14]

Courtesy of Davis and McCrum family descendants

Andrew Claycomb (1812-1886). Born in Kentucky, he was twenty-four years old when his family settled in Warren County and remained there for the rest of his life. Upon his death, the *Monmouth Review* said he "was well-known among the early settlers and was esteemed by them." Tom Davis called him "Father."

The Claycombs saw to it that the boys went to school during the winter months. At first it was private schooling, but public schools were soon organized. By 1850 Warren County schools were enrolling over four hundred children.

In the rugged environment of the farm, Tom and Frank Davis learned the skills and disciplines required. They cared for stock, their feed, tack, and shelters. Tom may have known something of his father's woodworking tools, but here the boys learned the tools of farming: scythes, hoes, plows, harrows. They loaded wagons and did what farmers had to do when something broke: fix it. They lived the annual rhythms of farm life—clearing new fields, preparing soil, planting seeds, tending gardens, pruning fruit trees, raising small animals. They protected the work animals and milch stock. They helped with the endless chores of harvest time, shipping, and putting up food. Successful farms relied on their own resources, so it paid to assume an attitude that problems could be solved by one's own initiative and effort.

Mary Ann Davis continued to live in Warren County. She married John Miller in 1841. She bore three more children but her first two sons remained with the Claycombs. Mary Ann was unlucky in her choice of husbands, for this one, too, died young and left her with very little. She was a widow once more late in 1848 with three young children. By 1850, when the census enumerators came around, they found Mary Ann sharing a household in Monmouth with her married 19-year-old daughter Emily, Emily's husband, and their infant child.[15]

At the Claycomb's, the same census found Tom and Francis, aged fourteen and twelve respectively, a nine-year-old named Sarah, whom the Claycombs had adopted, and five other people, only one of whom was over twenty years old. One of the Claycomb's nieces, Amanda, was nineteen and the mother of a two-year-old and an infant. A boy of seventeen may have been another indentured or orphaned child.

Andrew Claycomb prospered. In 1855 he commissioned a building to be erected in the tiny commercial district of Monmouth. It was on the public square not far from the courthouse. He must have felt that investing in the growing town would profit him. In 1857 he was building what the *Monmouth Atlas* called "a substantial and beautiful residence on the Rosenbaum property" in Monmouth.[16]

Tom and Frank witnessed Claycomb's growing business diversification. With a "substantial" residence, Claycomb had attained at least the middle class. Stories that have passed down through the Davis family say that the Claycombs regarded the boys with warmth and affection, not as a cold bargain for servitude. As an adult, Tom Davis referred to Claycomb as "Father" and sent him gifts. In later years, Tom and Frank both wore a path between Boise and Monmouth. The boys were in a supportive setting as they learned how progress could be made by long years of hard work in one place, the judicious application of modern ideas, sober self-discipline, and the careful investment of one's gains.[17]

Another pioneer of the Illinois frontier, Abraham Lincoln, had set up his law practice in the state capital of Springfield, southeast of Monmouth. Having rather more of the Appalachian spirit in his makeup than the entrepreneurial spirit of north Illinois, he made it his work during the 1840s and 1850s to advance a career in politics. He traveled the state, getting himself known. He visited the Claycomb establishment—Claycomb being a strong supporter—and passed some of his time entertaining the children on the place.[18]

During the 1850s, the question of slavery increasingly threatened the union of the states. The Republican party selected Lincoln as its candidate for president in 1860. If elected, he pledged, he would halt the spread of slavery. After his election, the southern states began to secede from the Union. South Carolina went first in December 1860. Federal troops in Charleston withdrew to Fort Sumpter, a small refuge in the harbor. The secessionist states established a Provisional Government of the Confederate States of America.

By this time, the Davis brothers were young men. They had left the sheltering home of the Claycombs and were living in their mother's household, as recorded in the 1860 census of Warren County. Tom was identified as a miller; Frank had no listed occupation.[19]

After his inauguration in March 1861, Lincoln ordered provisions sent to Fort Sumpter. On April 12, the Confederates opened fire on the Fort, and the War Between the States began. Three days later, Lincoln called for 75,000 volunteers. Rumors spread that he would soon call for 200,000 more. In Monmouth, the young men of the town poured into the courthouse square to organize a military company and defend the Union. The *Monmouth Atlas* listed their names. One of them was F.M. Davis.[20]

But in May, when troops were mustered out of Monmouth and Peoria, neither F.M. Davis nor Thomas Davis was among them. The two indentured boys of Andrew Claycomb had taken another direction in life.

Chapter Two

IDAHO

B y the spring of 1861, crossing the great American plains from east to west was something less the ordeal than it once had been. Thousands of wagon wheels had defined the path, eliminating guesswork. A telegraph line was advancing across Nebraska parallel to the Platte River "road." The line would put the Pony Express, which carried mail between Missouri and California, out of business. It was even possible to ride a stage to the Continental Divide, as Mark Twain did that year on his way to Salt Lake City. Some travelers could make thirty to forty miles a day.[1]

Still, making the journey required money and planning. Tom and Frank Davis arranged to travel with a company of like-minded men headed for golden opportunities in the West. By March, when Monmouth's public square filled with would-be privates, the brothers' plans were most likely well advanced. It is tempting to imagine that while Tom was away from Monmouth on some errand that day in March, Frank impetuously signed the Army roster. Perhaps Tom returned and persuaded him to stick with the plan they had made before the war began.

Andrew Claycomb, for reasons of enterprise or fondness or both, helped equip and outfit his boys with a wagon, mule team, and supplies. Opportunities for gold, land, and business were to be had in the West, it was clear. Like newspapers elsewhere in the country, the *Monmouth Atlas* published letters home from earlier emigrants about these possibilities. News, not always accurate, often was spectacular.

Although the brothers had returned to the household of their mother by 1860, the experience engendered in them no particular desire to remain. Opportunity may have pulled them westward, but unhappy realities at home might have been worth leaving.[2]

If Tom or Frank wrote letters home with an account of their trip, these have not been found. Early Idaho histories usually contained short biographies of the state's founding citizens, the ones who had done well. These biographies mention the Davis journey west, but contain few details.[3]

The accounts say that the company consisted of 75 men but do not mention the departure or join-up point. If Tom and Frank left from Monmouth, it was a day or two to the east bank of the Mississippi River and the rowdy port town of Oquawka. From there, it was downriver towards Hannibal and St. Louis or upriver to crossing places such as Keokuk, Iowa. Continuing west, it was another 250-300 miles to the Missouri River and Council Bluffs, Nebraska, or St. Joseph, Missouri, towns from which emigrants "jumped off" on a ferry to cross the river. Then it was on to the Platte River road and westward.

Overland travelers followed the Platte and North Platte rivers across Nebraska and then crossed Wyoming. The Davis group arrived at South Pass, near the Wyoming-Idaho border, some time in June. From this place onwards, water flowed toward the Pacific Ocean. Near the pass, the trail forked. The party could proceed toward Ft. Bridger or take a more northerly sixty-mile shortcut called Sublette's Cutoff to Fort Hall, a small trading post. The company encountered a group of Mormons at South Pass who led them to believe that from Fort Hall, they should continue north to the Lemhi Valley, where they could take an Indian trail over Idaho's central mountains and soon reach the gold fields of Orofino and Pierce.[4]

During this particular summer, Fort Hall, without any military protection, had been abandoned because of Indian attacks. Experienced men who might have known the truth about conditions on the Indian trail were not at hand. The travelers proceeded to old Fort Lemhi, a Mormon settlement begun in 1855 and later abandoned by Mormon authorities. Here, they encountered men ready to spring the trap set by their partners at South Pass.

These men portrayed the Indian trail as too rough, too steep, too impossible for wagons. To help the travelers out, they said, they would gladly buy the wagons. The proffered prices revealed just how badly Tom Davis and the others had been duped. For $5, they could sell their $500 outfits or leave them behind. Tom Davis persuaded his comrades to load their horses and mules with whatever they could carry, then pile the rest on the wagons and burn the lot, depriving the scoundrels of such ill-gotten goods. Among other items, Tom kept Harriet Claycomb's gift of the Bible. It was a bitter introduction to the measure of men in the West.

After setting the fire well and hot, the party turned their backs to it and set off on the trail known today as the Southern Nez Perce Trail. The horses, not used to heavy packs, gradually settled down, and the party climbed the high passes and steep canyons of central Idaho. On this point, the Mormons had been honest. One day the men found the body of a white man, pierced with arrows, along the trail. Alarmed and much depleted of their supplies, the party reached Elk City, Idaho, in July—along with a snow storm.[5]

A swarm of prospectors in Elk City had just organized a mining district that June. By the end of August, the men of the Davis party were amidst a thousand miners hoping to strike their fortunes. Word came of a "fabulous" gold strike in Florence. Much of the population rushed to get there early, abandoning Elk City. While some men managed to take values of up to $100 per day, the majority had to settle for something considerably less.[6]

People were still arriving in October, along with the cold and snows of what was to be a severe and early winter. One future Boisean, who survived that Florence winter and later became a friend of Tom Davis, described Florence:

The scene we beheld when we reached the summit camp was weird and depressing. It was dark and snowing, and in that strange bivouac a few men were cooking supper around miserable little fires. Others were rolled up in their blankets asleep on the snow. Many of them made a business of packing supplies on their backs into Florence, for which they received 50 cents per pound. In the gray of a dismal [next] morning with a storm, half sleet and snow...we faced the 18 miles that lay between us and the great gold placers of Florence...A cluster of log cabins, half buried in the snow, constituted the town of Florence.[7]

The placers were on the shoulder of a mountain 10,000 feet high. "The air is so very light," wrote prospector Elijah Bristow, who also carried a supply of woolen socks to sell, "that a person can scarsely breathe at times." Those who had rushed to Florence had to decide whether or not to remain for the winter. Snow would close the mountain passes, and there would be no traffic, supplies, or fresh food until spring. Tom and Frank Davis wisely spent the winter in Walla Walla.[8]

The winter in Florence and the region in general proved so harsh that many men died of exposure and starvation. Tom and Frank had a hard enough time in Walla Walla. People burned furniture and fence posts to keep themselves warm. Cattle starved, unable to paw through frozen snow. Some miners suffered from scurvy. A pathetic letter home from a Florence miner named James Hutton said, "Sickness here is caused by bad whiskey and worse company...I would like to be at home and see all of you and have some apples etc to eat."[9]

The Florence placers were shallow. They had been worked out in a single season. Those who had not spent the winter there had little reason to return in 1862, especially when men showed up on the streets of Walla Walla with gold dust from Auburn in Baker County, Oregon. These fresh diggings promised a fresh chance, especially for the early comers. So the tide of miners and the Davis brothers turned south to Auburn.[10]

Auburn came to life in April, quickly swelling with six thousand people. In June, three men called a meeting to plat the town. Someone sank a hole looking for a well site and found a claim instead. In hours, the whole townsite was taken up for claims. Soon the main street was a mile long. Alas, true employment was available only for a thousand men. A few claims were rich. Most were not.[11]

Reports entered Auburn that summer of the progress of the war between the states, including the fact that Abraham Lincoln had signed the Homestead Act. After the southern states had seceded from the union, their opposition to such an act had been eliminated. The new law allowed a person to settle on 160 acres of unoccupied public land. By cultivating it for five years, they could own it. Heretofore, public lands had been for sale for $1.25 an acre.[12]

By fall, Auburn was getting dull. Luckily, news of a gold strike in the Boise Basin promised another excitement. "I must admit," wrote Bristow, "I have the feaver, badly...There has been a rush to Boise. I am off...if it does not snow before Thursday." Among the rushing crowd were Tom and Frank Davis. They headed out and arrived in Idaho City around November 1862.[13]

In January 1863, Bristow wrote, "The Boisee Mines are a fact...I think there will be an immence amount of Dust taken out there next Season... There is about two-thousands men there now...there was reports in circulation of new discoveries on the headwaters of the Pyette...Fruit was selling .80 to $1.00..." He cautioned his friends back home, "I don't wish any of you to get excited about the Mines from anything I may write for this is decidedly a precarious life to live."[14]

Nevertheless, wrote Frank Coffin about Boise Basin, people "found what they were looking for. From grass roots to bedrock the golden dust was there in quantities sufficient to satisfy the wildest dreams of avarice."[15]

This time, prospectors were happy to stay through the winter. In Idaho City, they built crude cabins and then made snowshoes and prospected the snowy gulches. Sherlock Bristol, William L. Ritchey, and others built twenty cabins in a group. One day, someone tried to dig a well nearby, as it was a lengthy walk to the creek. At about eighteen feet, the fellow observed flecks of gold. A bucketful panned out at about $2.50. Suddenly, the cabin sites were worth real money; Bristol later claimed he took $300,000 from his. Such was the luck of early arrivals.[16]

Tom and Frank Davis had arrived early enough at this El Dorado to share in the luck. Bristol said that he, with Ritchey and Davis were partners in a claim "six miles from Steamboat Springs." Over the winter, claims were yielding anywhere from $10 to $200 a day. As the winter progressed, water became scarce. For a payoff of $20, men were willing to load flour sacks and carry them on their backs to a source of water several hundred yards away. Some claims were so promising that their owners announced they were not for sale at any price. They planned to work the claims themselves even if it took two years to do it.[17]

Tom and Frank Davis got acquainted with Bristol, Ritchey, George Ellis, and others who would later populate Boise City. They shook hands with Ritchey and Ellis as partners in at least one claim. It was said that Tom had a stake worth at least $5,000 by the time he left Idaho City. During January of 1863, 4,000 prospectors poured into Boise Basin. February came, and the influx continued. From California, Oregon, and Lewiston, miners arrived by the hundreds every day.[18]

Of the mining camps he had seen to date, Tom Davis sensed that the Boise Basin had some staying power. Prospectors were discovering quartz lodes; these would require several years to finance and work. The gold field was large and generous, supporting three distinct mining districts and towns to go with them.[19]

When the weather was too severe to mine or prepare ditches and sluices for the coming spring freshets, miners got together and talked. Ritchey recalled one of the storytellers, whom they called Cap McKay:

He was an old Hudson's Bay trapper and had trapped in Boise Valley. He said it was a beautiful valley and I got enthused over his description. So the night I went to see Tom Davis, I said to him, "Tom, let's go down to Boise and take up a ranch." He said, "I'll go [with] you." [20]

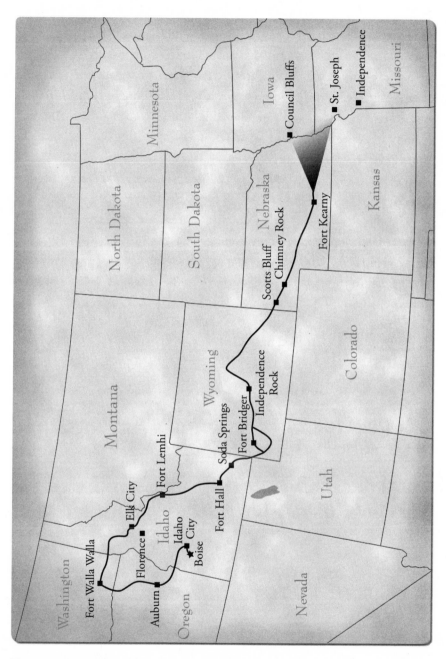

The way to Boise. Tom and Frank Davis, traveling in a group of 75 men, took an unusual route to the gold strikes in the Northwest, crossing the central Idaho mountains between old Fort Lemhi and Elk City.

Everything added up for Tom: a large population, prospects for several years of mining, the obvious market for fresh food and gold to pay for it, the near impossibility of shipping fresh fruit and vegetables from long distances by pack trains, the bane of scurvy. Trained by Farmer Claycomb, Tom Davis knew what to do. Tempered in mining camps, he had observed the way of water in the arid West. He saw how a simple ditch brought water to where it was needed.

On February 4, Tom Davis and William Ritchey walked out of Idaho City, leading their pack horse through four feet of snow along Cottonwood Creek and gradually onto bare ground. Reaching the lower foothills north of the Boise River valley, they camped overnight. The next day, they regarded the scene before them, marked by the Boise River and its thread of trees. Following the creek, they arrived at the river and staked a claim.[21]

— *Chapter Three* —

BOISE

Tom Davis and William Ritchey weren't the only ones in Idaho City who thought the Boise Valley had potential. That winter of 1862-63, some fifty men brought three hundred mules and horses down to the valley to feed on its green and snow-less pasture. Cap McKay himself had a shelter near the river about four miles below the Davis claim. Dave Littel, who happened to own a wagon, settled upstream, close to where Boise River debouched from its canyon and not far from the Warm Springs, where geothermal water sent plumes of steam toward the winter sky. In the following months, others staked claims on both sides of the river for a dozen miles. By common parlance, the claims were called "places" or "ranches."[1]

Mindful of the Homestead Act and other laws regarding land, men estimated parcels of about 160 acres each and marked their boundaries. Partners Tom Davis, William Ritchey, Frank Davis, and George Ellis laid ambitious plans and got busy. They required a cabin, a diversion ditch, and seeds.

Erecting the cabin fell chiefly to Frank Davis and William Ritchey, aided by Tom and others when they were in the valley. The prospect was not without risk, as they had reason to think that unfriendly Shoshoni Indians might be in the area. In March, miners from Placerville, angry about Indians who had stolen horses, volunteered under the leadership of miner Jeff Standifer to drive the Indians from the Basin and wipe them out entirely, if possible. The miners passed through Littel's place near Warm Springs and headed several miles south to Indian Creek, where they saw eighteen Indians and killed them. For another six weeks, they continued to slaughter men, sometimes women and children, whenever they found them.[2]

The cabin builders may have feared the Indians, but they didn't join the miners. Instead, Frank Davis and Ritchey rented Littel's wagon to haul cottonwood logs to their cabin site. Using the biggest logs for the walls, they split others for the roof and placed them flat-side down. Each time they returned to the river to collect another load of logs, they climbed whatever high point was available and scanned for possible trouble. They covered the roof with rye grass and dirt and left the floor in dirt.[3]

Ritchey hewed the door from one cottonwood log and made hinges. He and Frank hung it on the cabin. Against Indians, they made a heavy bar for the door and carved no windows in the cabin except for small peepholes along the roof. Fourteen by sixteen square feet, this cabin became the first island of hospitality, sociability, and planning for what would soon become Boise City.[4]

Tom Davis began digging his ditch, a project requiring substantial labor. He negotiated with his neighbors Tom Slater, John McClellan, and W.L. Thompson, offering them the use of water to irrigate their own ground if they would do part of the work. They "totally failed" to deliver the promised help. Many years later, when these men claimed a water-right interest in the canal, Davis apparently was still rankled by their poor grasp of mutual benefit, and, during a court proceeding, set the record straight.[5]

Davis began the ditch from a point on the north bank of the river about a mile and a half upstream and brought it toward his own claim, aided by the partner named George Ellis. It was four feet deep and six to eight feet wide. By June, it was in service, although Davis knew it would need a headgate the next year. As he recalled years later, "It was a new country

Courtesy of Davis and McCrum family descendants

Frank Davis (1338-1891). Two years younger than Tom Davis, Frank had a similar devotion to hard work, diversified businesses, and progressive ideas. His Locust Grove Dairy was the first in Ada County to take orders via telephone.

and hard to get the ground in shape to irrigate, and then we increased it [the length of the ditch] every year."[6]

Later in the summer, when water ran low, he dammed the river to guide the water into the ditch. He didn't know it then, but this ditch was to become a long-lasting source of water for irrigating crops and town lots, water power for a flour mill, and a conduit for sewage out of town.[7]

With the gold from their claim, Davis ordered seeds from Portland. From there, mail and other freight went up the Columbia River to the Umatilla landing, then three hundred miles on trails to Idaho City and Boise. In due course, 2,500 pounds of seed potatoes arrived on a pack train, along with melon and cabbage seeds, corn, and onions. The freight alone cost 33 cents a pound.[8]

The partners planted and cultivated, the ditch brought water, the seeds grew. By sheer investment of sweat and labor, Tom Davis tackled the contours in the land so that ditch water could flow by gravity to his rows of vegetables. By all the evidence of their lives up to this summer and afterwards, both Tom Davis and his brother had powerful appetites for work.

In March, President Lincoln signed a bill creating the Idaho Territory. When this happy news reached the Davis-Ritchey cabin, Tom and Frank told their friends how Lincoln had visited the Claycomb farm years before when he was circulating around western Illinois, building his political network. Decades later, this story survived with the added detail that Lincoln had played marbles with Claycomb's young boys.[9]

Idaho's territorial status acknowledged just how much the Union government valued Idaho's gold. It strengthened the Union cause, stabilized its economy, shored up its credit, and financed the war. Settlers, miners, and Oregon Trail emigrants, on the other hand, merely hoped the government would bring federal protection against angry Indians.[10]

The U.S. Army, which had known for some time that a combination of armed miners and hostile Indians in the Boise Basin would not be good, prepared to set up a post. On June 8, 1863, Major Pinkney Lugenbeel, who had built other military forts in the West, left Fort Walla Walla with

ISHS 1900-24

Idaho City - Boise stage. The coach prepares to leave Idaho City for Boise. This fine-weather trip was unlikely to encounter a snowstorm, washout, or rockfall, events more likely when Tom and Hester Davis ran The Star roadhouse in the early days of the toll road.

several infantry companies and a detachment of cavalry to build another one. They arrived in Boise Valley on June 28 and received a cordial welcome from the thinly stretched string of men trying to raise food along the Boise River.[11]

The Davis-Ritchey cabin became the gathering place as Lugenbeel scouted the area and decided on the best place for the fort. By July 4, he had made up his mind, choosing ground on a low foothill near where Tom Davis and William Ritchey had stopped on their way from Idaho City. The views of the valley and horizon to the south were superb, and flat ground lay just below the site. Hay for the army horses was available on a convenient island in the Boise River, the same place the detachment had camped on its first night in the valley. Timber and water were plentiful just to the north, and the fort would need a good sawmill site. Lugenbeel reserved acreages for all these military needs.[12]

Between Fort Boise and the north boundary of Tom Davis' claim lay a flat sagebrush plain. The fort was an anchor of security in the valley and gave the settlers a substantial boost of confidence. The fort and its personnel also constituted a new market for food, services, and commerce. It quickly became obvious that town-type services would bring town-type people, and that they would all, therefore, need a town.

The logical place for a town site lay between the Fort and the claims on the river. On July 7, several men gathered at the Davis-Ritchey cabin, laid out a plat, and called it Boise City. The main east-west streets ran three-fourths of a mile north of the river and parallel to it. Sherlock Bristol, who presided over the meeting, said the incorporating group consisted of seventeen people and included a few army officers.[13]

Someone took a survey chain, probably borrowed from Lugenbeel, and staked ten blocks, five on each side of what they called Main Street. Each block had an alley and six lots on each side of it. The lots were 50 feet wide and 122 feet deep. Main Street had plenty of space for heavy traffic: pack trains, freight wagons, prospectors' mules, and emigrant wagon trains with their oxen and other stock. The incorporators distributed lots among twenty people and wrote their names on each lot of the plat. Pinkney Lugenbeel wrote his daughter, "I believe they have given me three or four lots," implying that he was a passive recipient. "If the town ever becomes worth anything, I will give the lots to you children." William Ritchey and Frank Davis each had their names on six lots. The names of Tom Davis and many others who had claimed land along the river were not on the plat.[14]

The general understanding was that alternate halves of each lot would be given to newcomers provided they "improved" it. As new sets of parallel streets were platted, and as Main Street elongated well beyond its first five blocks — which occurred within a few weeks — all it took to acquire a lot beyond the "thickly settled" portion of the town was to build a house upon it. As people came and went, ownership quickly passed out of the hands of the original twenty "owners," who had given, sold, or forgotten about their lots. Very obviously, the aim of the incorporators was to attract business and people, not profit from land sales. By the time Ada County began collecting property taxes in 1867, few of the people named on the first plat still possessed the property.[15]

The city's founders, wrote James Hawley in his history of Idaho, were of two types: those who just happened to be in transit between the valley and the Boise Basin gold fields and those with genuine faith in the venture. Farmers like Tom Davis already had expressed their faith by planting seeds.

Now, merchants like Henry C. Riggs, James Agnew, and Benjamin DuRell set up tents on their lots, took note of more lasting building materials in nearby pine forests and sandstone ledges, and indulged their own appetites for work.[16]

Incorporator Henry Riggs had proposed the name "Boise." He and the others began the strategic work of diverting merchants and other businessmen from their rush to Idaho City and Boise Basin. They made freighting trips to Portland do double duty as recruitment opportunities. The Boise group must have come across as an affable and trustworthy bunch, for they made an important catch just a few days after creating the plat. They persuaded Cyrus Jacobs, on his way to Idaho City to open a store, to pitch his tent instead on one of Boise's Main Street lots. After that, it was one "first" after another: hotel, blacksmithy, saloon, livery stable, bank, school, church, wedding, baby.[17]

Jacobs proved to be among those pioneers who, along with Tom and Frank Davis and many others, remained in Boise and invested in it wholeheartedly. At first they simply intended to grow their own businesses. Very soon they realized that collaborating with one another was a powerful way to create new opportunities for themselves and the town as a whole.

The rest of that hot summer was busy everywhere in the valley. Overland travelers, learning that a new townsite had popped up, made a path from the desert along what would eventually become Boise Avenue down to the "Eden" of the valley floor. Not far from Tom Davis' place, wagons splashed across the river or took the ferry established near it by John McClellan. Considering the travelers' needs to rest, refresh livestock, and re-supply, the main street of Boise became a de-facto part of the Oregon Trail.[18]

The "Boise City Original Townsite" eventually contained 140 blocks. The founders reserved whole blocks for public buildings. North-south streets ranged between First to Sixteenth streets. The northern edge reached the Fort, and the southern edge ended at Front Street, where Tom Davis' land began.

Major Lugenbeel's priorities dovetailed nicely with those of the new town builders. He needed construction material. Within three weeks, he had a sawmill running at Robie Creek, using mule power in the absence of water. He set up a lime kiln for bricks. As no road existed between the sawmill and the fort, he built one in August using civilian labor. The road followed Cottonwood Gulch, cut high above the stream.[19]

At the fort, buildings went up to house the soldiers and civilian employees. The bakehouse was an early priority. Horses needed barns and a corral. A salute to the anticipated permanence of the fort was a decision to house the officers in sandstone dwellings. Lugenbeel opened a quarry at a mesa called Table Rock east of town. In the face of desertions among the soldiers—many to Idaho City, where they could make $50 a day instead of $13 a month as soldiers—Lugenbeel hired civilian wage laborers when they had no better opportunities in Boise Basin. The mingling of military and civilian personnel made for fluid travel between Boise City and the Basin, the rapid spread of news, and the circulation of gold between the two places. By fall, Boise had a population of about 725 people.[20]

Tom and Frank Davis involved themselves with a toll road to Idaho City. Merchants and food suppliers all required a direct route between Boise and Boise Basin. Lugenbeel's first few miles to McRay's Gap and the sawmill on Robie Creek were a good start on the 36-mile road, but it was famously rugged and rocky, subject to washouts, the scene of high risk, dreadful accidents, and drowned horses. It needed serious investment. After winding up and down the high ridges shouldering Shaw Mountain to Robie Creek, the road followed Moore's Creek to Idaho City. On good days, the journey between Boise and Idaho City took nine hours. The first Territorial legislature and later the Ada County commissioners authorized toll-road franchises as a way to finance improvements.[21]

Some combination of Davis-Ritchey resources set about building a two-story roadhouse several miles from Idaho City on the bank of Moore's Creek in 1863. Variously called Davis & Ritchey's, The Star, and Fifteen-Mile House, travelers and freighters could spend the night, eat cooked meals, and exchange animals for fresh teams. The location gave the name to "the Davis Canyon" when travelers described the road. Frank Davis managed the place and lived there part of the year. He sometimes found himself on call to determine the passability of certain road segments after spring floods or slides. But his movements were fluid, too, as he ranged in both directions from the roadhouse to claims in Boise Basin and to the busy ranch in Boise.[22]

At Tom Davis' place, work turned to the first harvest. Tom and other ranchers hired wage labor and freighters when they could—or did it themselves when they couldn't. Melons, onions, corn, cabbages, and potatoes had to be cut or dug up, kept cool, loaded on wagons, and hauled the rugged miles to Boise Basin, where many among 16,000 people gladly spent some of their gold on Davis produce. Tom and his partners also cut wild hay, which they hauled to Idaho City and sold for $200 a ton. The partners cleared $12,000 that first year. They had enlarged their capital and laid plans on how to invest it in 1864.

- *Chapter Four* -

APPLES

When the several thousand Red June apple trees arrived at the Davis place, the work of planting them required the cooperative effort of all the partners: Tom Davis, George Ellis, Frank Davis, and William Ritchey. Frank's association with the orchard was to outlast that of the other partners. Ellis sold his interest to Tom and decided to homestead northwest of the townsite. His share of the partnership had consisted of 99 acres just upstream and adjacent to Tom's claim. William Ritchey sold his one-fourth undivided interest to the other partners in August 1867. After that, people called it the "Davis Brothers' orchard."[1]

Tom lengthened his irrigation ditch and built the headgate at the river diversion. Later, he installed a water wheel to lift water from the ditch to direct it to some of his land. It would take at least two years before the trees bore fruit, so he continued growing watermelons, cabbage, and the other crops he had raised earlier. At some point, he started growing berries. The original cover of rye grass on his land disappeared as acre after acre was leveled, watered, and cultivated.[2]

The townsite incorporators kept up their campaign to make Boise into a real city. One day James Reynolds stopped in front of Riggs & Agnews' store on Main Street and asked the way to Idaho City, where he intended to set up a newspaper. The two men dropped everything and gathered others to meet Reynolds. They persuaded him to end his journey right there. A real city needed a newspaper. He opened the *Idaho Tri-Weekly Statesman* and published its first issue on July 26, 1864.[3]

H.C. Riggs, whose pre-Boise experience included two years as mayor of Corvallis, Oregon, could see plainly — as did most of the ambitious Boiseans — that the Territorial Capitol, which Congress had designated at Lewiston when it created Idaho Territory, no longer belonged there. Lewiston's prospects, as it was widely said in Boise, were "declining."[4]

His cohorts elected Riggs to the House in time for the convening in Lewiston of the second session of the Territorial Legislature, which could move the capital if it wished. Riggs' backers gave him strong support, and he made no effort to apologize for his unabashedly pro-Boise mission. They all talked up Boise as the "future capital of Idaho." The newspaper editor of the *Idaho World* in Idaho City, not a Riggs supporter, wrote:

> *...he would make a useful member [of the Legislature] if he were not troubled with "Territorial Capital" and "Boise City" on the brain. The only things he has asked for yet for Boise City are the Territorial Capital, a Branch mint, an Assay office, a distributing Post Office, and a division of Boise County and the location of the county seat at that place.*[5]

In the end, Boise got everything on Riggs' list except the branch mint, which no place in Idaho got. The territorial capital, the county seat, the assay office, and a post office were synonymous with new reasons for commerce, and therefore the city, to grow. The blocks and lots began to fill up. The role of the townsite incorporators began to diminish, and the buying and selling of real estate itself became a commercial business.[6]

James Reynolds (and, after 1872, the newspaper's next owner Milton Kelly) became part of the city's promotional machine. He knew the paper would be read widely, not only in Idaho Territory but elsewhere in the West. Aside from advertising the city to the outside world, he also promoted internal improvements and praised the accomplishments of hard-working citizens. In August 1864, he was celebrating his city's role as the agricultural pillar of the Boise Basin mines. In August 1864, he reported that "luscious watermelons in great abundance" had gone up to Idaho City. Vegetable wagons went directly from the valley to the Basin, where produce went to vegetable brokers, restaurant kitchens, and whoever stood on the corner ready to buy.[7]

Tom Davis was involved in selling town lots or, in some cases, facilitating the business of the townsite company. Receipts that were collected on behalf of the townsite went into a fund for street and other improvements. Other sales were simply business. In August 1864, he and William Ritchey sold three lots at the corner of Ninth and Bannock streets for $300 in gold. He sold another three lots at Forth and Washington to John A. O'Farrell in October. From Block 5 of the first plat, Davis and Ritchey sold for $50 one of the lots originally distributed to Ritchey. Sales continued into 1865, and by this time, property often included buildings. One such lot in Block 6 brought Davis $500. Another fronting on the north side of Main Street in Block 4 brought $1,900 for only part of the lot.[8]

One of the few photographs of early Boise City shows a sign painted with an image of a horse outside the establishment of blacksmith G.W. Stilts. For his lot on Main Street, Stilts paid Tom Davis and William Ritchey $2,000 "in hand" for his 25-foot frontage and improvements on the north side of Main Street.[9]

Between 1863 and 1867, Boise City had no municipal government. Despite the efforts of the Territorial Legislature, Boise voters rejected a charter in 1864 and twice in 1866 when they elected people who pledged that, if elected, they would not take the oath of office or serve. The general sentiment was that city government would require taxes, and that taxes would be a waste of money. They felt that, despite occasional episodes of claim jumping, the townsite company was managing the sale of lots and keeping up with growth. Entrepreneurs had improved the toll road between Boise and Idaho City. Street and lawn trees had arrived in Boise as early as 1864, along with a shipment of cats and chickens. There was even a hospital, where sick miners and others were cared for kindly until their last days. Although law and order had been in short supply during

Boise's first year or so, things had settled down, aided by the presence of county officers such as a sheriff.[10]

Matters changed when the United States surveyed the lands of Idaho Territory, a task it had postponed until after the Civil War. Under the leadership of Lafayette Cartee, whom the legislature appointed Surveyor General, and his assistant Peter Bell, the survey commenced in 1866. Beginning at an ancient volcano plug, Initial Point, in the desert southwest of Boise, the surveyors measured out townships and ranges, each divided into thirty-six square-mile sections.

The settlers on the town lots were technically squatters on the public lands until someone with proper authority filed the plat with the Government Land Office in Boise. For anyone to obtain clear title, it was necessary that Boise have a mayor and council with the authority to file the plat. An election in November 1867 produced another winning mayor who refused to take his oath, so the "city fathers" asked attorney Henry Prickett, who had been acting as a notary public for deed transactions and whose calm demeanor engendered trust, to take office and file the plat. Which he did. Before he resigned two months later, he regularized the townsite fund to finance city improvements and collected $600 for it. This appears to have ended the responsibilities of the townsite company.[11]

People who lived outside the townsite managed to vote in these chartering elections, even though they technically weren't qualified. Whatever sentiments the Davis group might have felt about it, they too were squatters and had to act to obtain their own titles. In addition, the survey corrected the boundaries of the 442-acre city plat on its south-east border, where it abutted Tom Davis' claim, and other claim boundaries.

Several of Tom Davis' land transactions in the next few years involved quit claims that rationalized his established lanes and garden fences with the corrected survey boundaries. Davis and James Slater, for example, exchanged quit claims in September of 1869 to make such adjustments. The lane between them eventually became the path to the Ninth Street Bridge, which crossed to the south side of the river.[12]

When Tom Davis made his own trip to the Land Office to obtain a patent, he filed under the Act of 1820, not the Homestead Act of 1862. He had ready cash to pay for his 153.7 acres at $1.25 each, and did so. Others who had staked claims in the valley early in 1863 obtained certificates bearing the same 1869 date, but, after Boise City's plat was given Certificate No. 1, Tom's was No. 2.[13]

Tom's apple orchard began bearing fruit in 1866 or 1867. Although it sometimes took robust effort to preserve the fruit in the face of frosts and pests, Tom was willing to expend it. During the many grasshopper plagues of the 1860s, he hired large forces of men to populate the orchard and shake the trees from 4 a.m. until late afternoon. The grasshoppers dined on the vegetation on the ground and Tom saved the trees.[14]

For white miners, the rush for gold in the Boise Basin began to abate between 1865-1870. Many left. Taking their place were Chinese men, many who had come to the West to build the transcontinental railroad. In 1870, the Census counted the population of the Boise Basin at 3,528, including 49.3 percent who were Chinese. Thus, the market for food remained steady enough, and the growing Ada County population added to it. By the time valley growers were harvesting big surpluses, they were well-equipped to search out markets at ever more distant mining camps.[15]

After buying out Ellis and Ritchey, Tom Davis planted other varieties of apples and fruits. He made vinegar and cider. He built a fruit drier in the middle of the orchard and experimented with dried apples, which extended the market during the winter months.

For Boise and Ada County, the 1870 census found that Tom Davis' agricultural establishment had the highest cash value of all the farms listed in the census. By this standard, he was the wealthiest farmer in the valley. He had four hundred improved acres and forty acres of woodlands, most likely those lands in the flood plain of Boise River. He was a major employer, having paid out $5,000 in wages and board in 1869. His machinery and equipment were worth $500. He owned two horses, seventeen mules and asses, and one milch cow; the value of this stock was $1,800. He had produced 1,500 bushels of spring wheat, 9,100 bushels of barley, and 1,250 bushels of Irish potatoes. At this time, the produce of his market garden was substantially more valuable at $1,000 than his "orchard products" at $100. The Census enumerator found his farm the only one in the county with a value greater than five figures, at $10,125.[16]

Tom had long since abandoned the cottonwood cabin with the peepholes near the roof. He had built a house nearer the river and closer to orchard operations. His "personal estate," as defined by the Census, was worth $1,800. In 1870, he was sharing the household with three other men, in all likelihood his employees or renters. [17]

Prior to the fort and the city, the only women in the Boise Valley were Native Americans. By 1870, white women had arrived in substantial numbers and became partners in households and farms. They commenced building the town in all the ways open to women to build. Frank Davis married one of them, but Tom had been too busy to keep company with women, much less marry.

— *Chapter Five* —

WOMEN

ester Corey arrived in Boise on August 18, 1864, on a wagon train arriving on the "tide of emigration that still flows in," as James Reynolds put it. She was twenty-two years old. She described herself and her brother, also on the train, as orphans but did not elaborate. Like Tom and Frank Davis, she must have felt that leaving "the States" was a better chance for life when little else compelled her to stay where she was.[1]

Born in Wyandot County, Ohio, near Upper Sandusky, Hester grew up in Mt. Pleasant, Iowa. She joined a wagon train led by Peter Smith, who, with his wife, took Hester under their protection. Mrs. Smith was a midwife, and she asked Hester to help a Mrs. Heffleman, who was pregnant and traveling in a spring wagon drawn by horses.[2]

The Hefflemans were bringing with them a herd of five milk cows, which traveled at the rear of the 150-wagon train with the other stock, tended by the young boys in the party. After crossing the Missouri River on a ferry at Omaha, Captain Smith kept them on the north side of the Platte River. When the train camped along a creek, someone milked the cows and set the milk cans to cool in the creek. After breakfast, the cans with leftover milk and cream were hung up at the rear of the wagon. By noon, the lurching of the wagons had turned it into butter.

When the train stopped for a midday rest near a stream, Hester and the other women brought out butter bowls and ladles. They washed the butter and salted it. "It was our only luxury, so we used it generously in making hot biscuits and for other cooking," said Hester. Buffalo chips fueled their fires.

Wagon travel had its other routines and anxieties. Hester slept in a tent with the Smiths and their two daughters. The summer of 1864 was known for its "millions of crickets" which had to be swept out of the tents before spreading the beds. When the train descended steep hills, the men tied the front and back wheels of the wagons together, then held ropes tied to the wagon sides to prevent the wagons from pitching forward. They all feared the Indians they met along the way, but Captain Smith was tactful with them. Wisely, he ordered the other men in the train not to speak to them.[3]

Near the Idaho-Montana border, Mrs. Heffleman gave birth to a girl and named her Idaho Montana Heffleman. Captain Smith led the train into Idaho near Dubois, and the group rested for two weeks. The company split, and a sizeable group headed north into Montana, while the others continued to Boise.

Two days before Hester's group appeared in Boise, Reynolds wrote that wagon "trains are passing every hour of the day, bound for the valleys below. Many spread their tents in the suburbs of town to recruit up and look about them for homes in our own beautiful and fertile valley." After Hester's group arrived, "the streets were fuller than usual of wagons and stock." Encouraging the emigrants to stay in Boise, the editor said, "There is no branch of business but needs more laborers," especially farm labor.[4]

Hester had entered Boise astride a horse, along with her brother, the Smiths, the Hefflemans, and eight or nine men who went ahead of the train to find a place to stop the wagons and pitch their tents. By this time, Boise's "suburbs" provided little food for stock, so the first order of business was to drive the cattle to the foothills to feed.

After some days of meeting people and making arrangements, Hester went to live with the Stewart family in the gulch northwest of Boise that

Hester Corey Davis (1842-1937). Hester crossed the plains in 1864, rode into Boise on a horse, and captured the heart of Frank Davis. After his death, she managed their dairy and stock enterprises. An admiring obituary said she was mentally sharp, a good businesswoman, and, despite her small size, could do "the work of a man."

now bears its name. The Stewarts had what Hester called a "double cabin," two large rooms with a covered breezeway between. Men bunked in one side, the family in the other. Just above them in the gulch was the Miller place. Hester became acquainted with Mrs. Miller, who was pregnant. Before she was due, the Millers moved to a house at Tenth and Main streets in Boise, taking Hester with them. Mrs. Miller soon had her baby, and Hester was an asset in the household.

That winter, Boise had about 1,600 people, the minority being women. Of these, single women were an even smaller minority, and therefore much appreciated for enhancing all social occasions. Hester attended a dance party, probably more than one. She may have been at the Overland House in mid-November, when "the elite of the city were in attendance," including ladies and gents from Idaho City. "And such a bevy of female loveliness. The Basin boys say they never saw the like." Hester didn't say which dance it was when she met Frank Davis, only that he happened to be in town, having left a hired couple in charge of the Star after the snows closed the road for stage travel.[5]

Wasting little time, Frank and Hester married on January 18, 1865 at the Star, where Reverend Newton from Idaho City performed the ceremony. "If I had taken years to pick out a husband," she said later, "I could not have found a better one." They lived at the Star, which was near one of the road's toll stations. Their living quarters at the two-story building were on the first floor, which contained two bedrooms, a sitting room, kitchen, dining room, and bar room. The cellar was below. Upstairs, customers slept in six beds arranged in one undivided room.[6]

Hester and Frank lived at the Star for several years. Their son Charles was born there in 1865, but by 1870, they had moved to Boise. Frank built a fine frame house on the south side of Grove Street between Seventh and Eighth streets, very near the old cabin he had erected with William Ritchey. One of their four boarders in 1870 was Hugh Pickel, a tin smith by trade and one of Frank's partners in various business ventures. With great pleasure, Frank and Hester dismantled the old cabin, burning one old cottonwood log at a time to warm their new house.[7]

She and Frank entered fully into the social life of the town. Hester had accumulated managerial skills running the kitchen at the Star, and in Boise she was known to handle an occasional catering job. When the captain at Fort Boise and his wife hosted one of the "splendid" winter dance parties at the Overland House hotel, Hester provided the supper "gotten up in delicious style" for a hundred couples.[8]

The Census that year estimated the value of Frank's real estate at $4,000 and his personal estate at $3,000. Some of Frank's land was located northwest of the townsite. Earlier in 1870, for $1,600 in gold coin, he had purchased 160 acres in what would eventually contain Elm Grove Park in Boise's North End. By 1880, the farm was valued at well over $10,000, and Frank's thirty milch cows produced over a thousand pounds of butter. His small orchard was in apple and peach trees, and the grasslands produced sixty tons of hay. By 1885, Davis was taking orders by telephone, the city's recent modern improvement, and delivering butter and cream all over town. The Claycombs had reason to be proud of both their boys.[9]

After Tom Davis had separated most of his interests from those of Ellis and Ritchey, he and Frank continued developing the orchard and finding markets for produce and fruit. This required travel to make market connections in Montana, northern Nevada, the Wood River, and the Owyhee mining country across the Snake River. Tom was ambitious and relished his work. In a later century, friends might have called him a workaholic. His friend at the newspaper teased him in print about being "the most incorrigible woman hater of us all," which implies that he didn't spend much time wooing women at dances.[10]

Still, Tom was hardly anti-social. He played the violin, enjoyed all things musical, and was a member of the city's band for many years. He played chess, eventually becoming organizer and president of the city's first chess club. He must have been good at spinning yarns, for one of them — a tale of how a character from Knox County in Illinois called "General Knox" named a set of quadruplets "Awful, Wonderful, Circumstance, and Fact" — was so memorable that Thomas Donaldson recalled it in his memoir, *Idaho of Yesterday*. When the weather was cold enough, Tom flooded one of his pastures for community ice skating. Tom's "problem" with women was simply that the right one didn't arrive in Boise until 1869.[11]

She was Julia McCrum. We know less about her journey to Boise than about Hester's. Her starting place was a small town called Galt in Ontario, Canada. On the Grande River, the settlement was the project of a man named William Dickson, who had purchased a 90,000-acre tract from the Six Nations in 1816. He saw great potential in the region for farming.[12]

Dickson at first named the town Shade's Mills after Absolom Shade, whom he had hired to manage his land. Dickson and Shade began soliciting relatives and acquaintances both close and distant to come and settle. One of Shade's distant relations was Julia McCrum's grandfather, Henry McCrum, located in the Lake Canandaigua country of New York State. He most likely was one of the Scots-Irish McCrums who had migrated from County Armaugh in North Ireland to Bristol, Massachusetts, shortly before the rebellion against England and then, as loyalists, had removed themselves from the conflict.[13]

His son, also named Henry McCrum, responded first to Shade and arrived in Canada in 1834, his father following later. By that time, Dickson had managed to establish a post office for the place. He named it and the town Galt, in honor of John Galt, a Scottish novelist and a commissioner of the Canada Company. To its agricultural service economy, Galt eventually attracted some industry, so that by the 1830s, Galt promoters called it "the Manchester of Canada."

Dickson also recruited in Scotland and England. He attracted Julia's other set of grandparents, William and Marion Batters, whose ancestral roots were in Etal, Northumberland, a county on the English side of the Scottish border. They left Enfield, England, where they were living when their daughter Marion was born, and went to Galt in 1832 to take up farming. Batters raised fine cattle and cream-colored horses, which he then exported to England. One of his customers was the English royal family. He built a "very fine cut stone house" of the same design as the old family home in Etal and gave it the same name, Bank Head. Later in Boise, Julia told stories about Grandfather Batters, whom she had known until he

Courtesy of Davis and McCrum family descendants

Henry McCrum (circa 1820-1879). The father of Julia McCrum Davis, Henry arrived in Galt, Ontario, in 1834, responding to recruitment appeals from Absolom Shade. This image is from a painted portrait.

died when she was six. For people who heard the story third- and fourth-hand, the upshot was that Julia was from a "fine English family" and was a "refined young woman of Galt." Julia's habitually gracious manner certainly supported this impression.[14]

By the time Julia's parents married around 1841, both the McCrum and Batters families were well established in Galt. Their first child died before Julia, the second, arrived on January 24, 1847. She grew up, in effect, the eldest of seven siblings, two girls and five boys. She and the older children were born in a house known as "the White House at the top of Queen Street," but when she was five, the family moved to a larger property on a hill. The children grew up attending Galt's public schools, romped with the family's pet dogs, and went to church on Sundays.[15]

As they reached adulthood, the McCrum siblings, influenced by the "Wander Lust," found opportunities across Lake Erie in the United States. Two of Julia's brothers, Henry and Richard, went to Indianapolis to work. Their mother, tiny of stature but able to wield considerable influence, never

Marion Batters McCrum (1822-1903). Mrs. McCrum kept the path between Galt and Boise open for visits to and from her daughter, Julia. She spent the winter of 1880-81 in Boise after her husband died. Julia's daughter Etta was in Galt in March 1900.

liked their leaving. When her husband died in 1879, she received some insurance money and used it to entice them back to Galt. She succeeded, and they bought a book and stationary business. Despite this outwardly sober enterprise, Henry led a life that provoked a descendent to write of him and his brothers, "The McCrum men were all gamblers...They believed every wildcat mining venture would turn into a real bonanza. None of their stocks did well for them."[16]

Mrs. McCrum had a public reputation as a woman of culture, "with wide sympathies and most amiable disposition." She also had a fierce sense of pride and a great love of Canada, the Crown, and all things British. With all that, she wasn't able to keep her children close to her Galt hearth. Three of them, including Julia, went off to Idaho.

One of Mrs. McCrum's Scottish friends was the wife of a surgeon who was being sent to Fort Boise in 1869. Mary Thibado suggested that Julia, then twenty-two, come along and stay with her for a visit in Boise.

Julia agreed. If she had not displayed a spunky or "venturesome spirit" heretofore, Julia proved to her mother and friends that she did indeed have one, for any view of Idaho Territory from Galt was the "wild west."[17]

The manner of her coming must have befitted the family of a military officer transporting his family to his post, but Julia didn't tell the story of the route she took. In Boise, the Thibados lived in town, and Dr. Augustus Thibado was the fort's chief surgeon. In August 1868, he was elected to serve as Ada County coroner. In 1870, the three Thibado children were three years, one year, and five months old respectively, which may supply some understanding as to why Mrs. Thibado valued Julia's extra hands around the house.[18]

Julia hadn't expected to become Mary's in-house babysitter and maid, but this soon became her unhappy predicament. In Boise, however, it was inevitable that tall auburn-haired bachelors would meet young unmarried women with a taste for adventure. Tom Davis met Julia, courted her, and they married on April 26, 1871, in the Thibado's house, witnessed officially by Dr. Thibado and Tom's good friend Charles Himrod. Tom was thirty-three years old, Julia twenty-four.[19]

Tom offered his bride a comfortable house surrounded by an apple orchard, a secure economic future, household help, and the social status that came with being the wealthiest farmer in Boise, a reliable citizen, and a successful pioneer. While Tom was still a bachelor, the newspaper editor painted a picture of the setting that Julia was about to enter:

> By industry [Tom Davis and Co.] have reclaimed and made their ranch the fit abode for man. Their young orchard is in a thriving condition and presents a pleasing appearance. It covers twenty acres, and is composed of apple, pear, peach, and plum trees, about fifty of which will bear the coming season. The peach trees are already filled with young peaches. They also have a patch of blackberries, of the Lawton variety... The Davis brothers bestow the greatest care upon their orchard, which in a few years will pay them tenfold for their labor. Every department of their ranch looks well.[20]

Among the few stories that offer an insight into the partnership of Tom and Julia Davis is one that affirms his work ethic and attention to detail. The night of their wedding was a cold one that threatened to freeze the blossoms off the apple trees. As the couple walked about the orchard together, Tom fretted about what steps he might take to protect his trees, distracted from the other important matter at hand. Julia is reported to have laughed and said, "Oh Tom, did you marry an apple blossom?"[21]

The Davis family oral tradition is that Tom and Julia were equal partners. Julia's heritage supplied her with an independent perspective on life, and she remained free to assert her own convictions. She embraced her new home city and lent her robust personal energies and Davis resources to community improvement and social charity. She shared the progressive impulses of her husband and others in building up Boise City.

The happy union of Tom and Julia seems to have divided the families of Tom and Frank. The two branches of the family are rarely mentioned together after Tom married, and the whispers down the generations say that Tom and Hester shared few if any mutual sympathies. Frank had partners other than his brother and always had his own irons in the fire. In 1871, for example, he and Hugh Pickel ordered a boring machine that they hoped would help them locate an artesian well for public use in downtown Boise or even find water for the arid lands between Boise and the Snake River. By the 1880s, Frank and Hester had moved west of town to live at their dairy (near today's State and Twenty-first streets), which became the center of their other land and livestock investments. The two Davis families were each esteemed in their social circles, but the circles seldom intersected.[22]

Chapter Six

MARION

On January 31, 1872, Julia and Tom Davis welcomed their daughter Marion into the world. They named her after Julia's mother and grandmother. The parents were utterly charmed by this child.

Marion was nearing two years old when Julia determined to take her east to show her off to her grandparents. She left Boise on November 10, 1873, as autumn was about to turn to winter. Most likely, she took the stage to Kelton, in 1869 the nearest station from Boise on the Central Pacific Railroad. Luckily, this particular winter would prove to be a mild one, with the road open and little or no snow. After the stage journey, which took several days, the eastbound train would take her at a quicker pace to other rail connections, ferries, and stages to the Claycomb's place in Illinois and from there to Galt.[1]

Tom stayed home, unable to see his way to a protracted absence from the orchard, the farm, and the various enterprises associated with them. He hated the separation from Julia and Marion, however, and counted every day she was gone.

The only letter that survives of all that Tom and Julia wrote to one another during their lifetimes is one that Tom wrote on Christmas eve while Julia was away on this trip. Aside from his anxiety over not hearing from her more often, and perhaps not knowing her exact location, considering the risks of travel, the letter shows him never at a loss for things to do and supplies a glimpse of his continuing relationship with his "father," Andrew Claycomb.

Boise City, December 24, 1873

My dearest Julia,
Considering that you are as glad to get a letter from me as I am from you, I will write you another. Tonight I would willingly pay you $200 a letter twice a week to hear from you and my baby, having been gone 44 days.

I have just scoured the kitchen floor and it looks as clean as a new pin. I keep everything clean except the dusting that I neglect to some extent. I am just through rendering out lard, had 10 cans, have got it nicely put away. Bob gets breakfast. I don't get up til breakfast is ready. We have warm bread every meal made of yeast powder. I get dinner and wash the dishes and have a great time scolding Bob to make him keep clean. I made about 40 lbs. of sausage meat and it is nice. We haven't killed a chicken since you left home. The women have offered to come and clean my house but I told them my house was the cleanest.

I set out 500 apple trees last fall and have got 4500 more to set out in the spring, which is a big job. I shall soon have to start in to get them all out this spring.

Dora Kesler is married tonight to a very wealthy man, poor Dora. She has ruined her future happiness if there was any for her.

The cow hasn't had a calf yet.

I had a sleigh ride this afternoon with Mrs. Missil and the old gray horse. We rode all over town. She said it was a great honor to her

*to ride with me. The school children laughed at us. She wanted to
know how you got on. I told her I had not heard from you for two
weeks. She said you would soon be home. She said she could not
leave Jo. Baby Nye says Marion can't have her locket. We haven't
had but 2 nights that were cold. The thermometer stood at zero at
5 in the morning. There is about 3 inches of snow.*

*I have just written home. I sent father 150 dollars. I sent Dolley a 10
dollar bill for a Christmas present and when you answer this tell
me everything the baby does and what she don't do. What would I
give to see you. If only you had written me at my home and then as
soon as you got to your home so I could have heard from you every
few days. How much more happy I would have been but I was so
disappointed. You know how restless I am when I thought you had
ought to written me. Put your own price on your dear letters and
send them on.*

Here, Tom wrote, "I remain ever your friend." But he crossed it out
and said instead, "Lots of kisses for your Self and Baby. I shall continue to
write often til I hear from you. Good by. Thomas Davis. As soon as I hear
from you I will send some more money."[2]

Tom must have worn his lonely heart on his sleeve, for when the
Statesman reported Julia's return late in February, the editor added, "Tom
is happy again."[3]

A year later, Tom and Julia welcomed their second child on March 7,
1875. They named him Thomas Jefferson after his father and soon called
him Tommy. He inherited his father's dark eyes and penetrating gaze.

Along with the Davis/McCrum household, Boise and Tom's stake
in it were growing, too. Later that year, telegraph service arrived in
Boise. Tom's 5,000 new trees had expanded his orchard and, in fact, he
needed more land. In 1874, he had bought 160 acres in Crane Gulch for
$4,500 and then planted another fruit orchard and more berries. He was
manufacturing vinegar and cider, drying apples, and pushing for sales
ever farther from Boise.[4]

One market was in Elko County, Nevada, where miners continued to strike promising ores. The growing population there inspired more agriculture and cattle production. John Sparks herded Texas longhorns into the region, and by the mid-70s, he was running 70,000 head and creating a cattle empire. On one of Tom's trips, it's likely that he became acquainted with Sparks, and the two must have talked cattle.[5]

In January 1876, the children of Boise were enduring one of the periodic rounds of disease that sometimes afflicted them. Roseola, also called rose-rash, was giving them sore throats and fever. The standard advice was to give the child warm tea and call the doctor. Marion Davis and her playmates, "Baby Nye" and Delphine Perrault, all happened to catch it. At one point, Dr. Stevens reported that "all were getting along nicely."[6]

But Marion's fever went out of control. She developed "inflammation of the brain and could not live...all hopes of her life are given up."[7] On February 4, she died.

Her funeral was at the Episcopal Church, where Reverend Bollard read the sad service. The child lay in her casket on a bed of flowers. The choir sang the final hymn, "Thy Will be Done." As the gathering rose to proceed to the Masonic Cemetery for the last solemn rites, Tom and Julia took their final look at Marion, hearts broken. Milton Kelly wrote, "We shall not attempt to portray their mighty grief."[8]

Sarah Tregay photo

Marion's gravestone in Pioneer Cemetery reads "Marion daughter of Thom. J. & Julia Davis Died Feb. 4th 1876 Aged 4 years 4 ds" followed by a worn inscription.

— *Chapter Seven* —

CATTLE

round 1879-1880, two of Julia's brothers came from Galt to visit. Like her own "visit," their's also transformed into permanent residence in Idaho. Nineteen at the time, Charles McCrum took a job as a clerk at Nye's drug store in Boise. One thing led to another, and with a partner, he established McCrum & Deary drug store in Boise in 1894. One of the store's specialties was Kimball's Sasparilla, named after his grandmother, Arathusa Kimball McCrum. His wife Jessie entered the same social strata as her sister-in-law, Julia. When the newspaper described the weekly comings, goings, and gatherings of Boise's "leading" families, she and Julia sometimes appeared on the guest lists at the same parties, musical entertainments, and receptions.[1]

Her other brother, John Edwin McCrum, known as Ed, lived in Julia's well-filled household, probably until he married. Ed was a few years older than Charles and started out as a grocery clerk. The household also contained another border and a servant named Emma Drake.[2]

Julia must have been glad for Emma Drake, for her children then included Tommy, three-year-old Harry and one-year-old Julia Etta. Between August 1880 and May 1881, the matriarch Mrs. McCrum herself, then a recent widow, also was in the house on a long visit from Galt. In

John Edwin McCrum (1857-1886). Julia's young brother, Ed, became the field partner of Davis & McCrum, a cattle operation in the Bruneau River country. Julia's fifth child, Edwin H., born in 1881, was given his name.

ISHS 14-128.27

November 1881, Julia delivered Edwin Horace, bringing the little Davis brood to four.[3]

Household help wasn't always available. Because Julia could afford it didn't necessarily mean she could get it. In addition, she competed with her husband when labor was scarce. The house's location near the river put her in close touch with emigrant traffic, which occasionally offered opportunities.

Julia already had earned a reputation as someone who took an active interest in new Boise arrivals, welcoming them while their tents were still pitched next to their wagons. Many travelers were notoriously exhausted, sick, or cash-poor at this far end of their arduous journey. It was Julia's generous practice—and that of others with farms and gardens along the route of the Emigrant Road—to load fruit and other produce onto wagons entering town.[4]

In August of 1882, the William Brabb family crossed into Boise from the trail, grateful to leave the blistering hot desert. Brabb wrote:

After leaving the river we came to ranches, and crossed one or two, and came into the road on the right side of Boise River. The land was fenced and planted to crops, orchards, and gardens. Boise City is called the City of Gardens, and they sure had plenty of them. We were told that we would think when we got to Boise that we were in the Garden of Eden. After passing through so much sagebrush and desert, it looked like Eden or some good place.[5]

His party decided to rest their teams, take up some work, and earn a little money. They camped near Government Island, still a hay reserve for Fort Boise (renamed Boise Barracks in 1879) and got work hauling baled hay to the fort. For this, it was worth their while to shod their mules and borrow wood at the lumber yard to help haul the hay. The boss hired one of the women in Brabb's group as a cook for the work camp.

I took the girls [his sisters] up to the city to see if they could get work for a few days. Everyone who wanted a girl wanted her steady. Didn't want to take one for less than 3 months, and wanted them for a year. A Mr. Davis wanted 2 girls for 2 or 3 months, then one girl steady right along...He would give 2 girls $6 per week till the heavy work was done, then he would pay one girl $5.00 per week.

We went to his house to get some apples. He keeps store in the city, has a large orchard and lots of apples going to waste though there were several white men and Chinese gathering them and drying. His wife offered to take Stella to nurse the children, and to pay her $1.50 per week.[6]

Many emigrants found the prospects in Boise promising enough to end their journey and stay put, but the Brabbs pushed on to Pendleton, so Julia probably got no help of Stella.

She might have wished that Tom's Chinese laborers had sisters. Chinese miners had made an early appearance in Boise in September 1865, when a "long train of celestials on the move in single file, supporting the middle of their long-handled shovels or a bamboo stick with pendant sacks of rice, chopsticks, rockers, and gum boots filed along Idaho Street" on their way to Idaho City.[7]

The Chinese eventually outnumbered white miners in the Boise Basin. Their skill at managing water made many of them wealthy. They earned respect among white miners and business owners; some invited partnerships with Chinese miners. But mining wasn't for every Chinese miner, as it hadn't been for every Caucasian miner. They established shops, bakeries, laundries, and blacksmith shops. Some wanted to garden.[8]

The gardeners must have struck up an affinity with Tom Davis. Most of the Chinese had farmed in Guangdong Province, where they had grown up. In Boise Basin, they managed to raise several harvests of green vegetables in a short three-month growing season. Eventually, they competed with growers in Boise, who made deliveries once or twice a week, by delivering produce door to door every day.[9]

Exactly how long before 1882 Tom Davis began hiring Chinese laborers has not been discovered, although he acquired a reputation as the first in Boise to "bring" Chinese gardeners to town. In 1882 the Chinese Exclusion Act prohibited any more Chinese from entering the United States. The Chinese population in Idaho began to shrink. As opportunities in the Boise Basin also shrank, some moved to Boise. Idaho laws constrained the rights of Chinese to own property, but Tom invited gardeners to lease the riverfront edge of his lands. Their intensively gardened plots—and door to door delivery—became an institution in Boise until well into the 1940s.[10]

Garden-leasing was only one of Tom's growing portfolio of enterprises. He had been considering the possibilities of a livestock business in the Bruneau River country south of the Snake River. He thought well enough of Ed McCrum to take a chance on him as the partner who would manage the field ranch. Ed had spent some of his early time in Idaho prospecting, apparently with the lack of success chronicled by later

ISHS 14-128.10

Tom and Julia's children. If photo was taken around 1885, Tommy would have been ten; Harry (on right), seven; Julia Etta, six; and Ed, four. The last child, Hazel, would arrive in 1888.

Government Island Ranch, circa 1910. Today occupied by Garden City, the scene from the Bench featured haystacks, Hereford cattle, and the Boise River. At right edge of the picture, a Boise Valley Interurban trolley comes around the bend.

McCrum family historians. But in December 1881, he married Mary Cartee, the youngest daughter of Lafayette Cartee, and was interested in more promising work.[11]

The two went into it as "Davis and McCrum." They set up the headquarters ranch at Bruneau and ranged cattle and horses in the southeast corner of Owyhee County south of Bruneau and into Elko County, Nevada. They set up a business account at Tom's store. The store had evolved in 1877 from Tom's Main Street fruit stand (two doors west of the stage office) to a grocery store where, among other things, he sold his own canned pickles and sweet corn, the recipes for which he perfected himself. The business grew into a well-stocked mercantile store that he co-owned with Charles Himrod. He and Himrod also ran freight teams between Boise and Kelton, so Tom was very familiar with the general territory and its ranching potential.[12]

Tom created the Bar O brand, and buckaroos referred to the Bruneau camp as "the Bar O outfit." Thus began the annual rhythms that marked

Courtesy of Davis and McCrum family descendants

Davis Ranch, near Cascade. Producing winter feed for cattle, as shown in this portrait of haying season at the Bar O, required a substantial investment in horses. Tom Davis eventually went into business raising and selling draft horses.

the cattle business: ranging stock in the Bruneau River drainages during the winter, raising feed, breeding and multiplying the herds, branding calves, driving the cattle to higher ground for the summer.[13]

None of Tom Davis' business records survive, but a few surviving journals from the Davis & Himrod store supply a store-counter view of the Davis & McCrum cattle business (and Tom and Julia's household purchases as well). The store sold just about everything: cloth, fresh and canned food, cord wood, household goods, seamless sacks, shoes, hats, tools, stock salt, pest poisons, white lead, nails, axle grease, candy, beer, cigars. At least once, Frank Davis came in with samples of fresh cheese to sell.[14]

At the store, account holders each had their own numbers. The clerk kept track of every item purchased each day and its price, and then settled up accounts at the end of the month. The Davis family account shows that store errands took place rather frequently, sometimes more than once a day. "Davis and McCrum," on the other hand, made infrequent stops that paint a picture of chores done while "in town."

Davis & Himrod Store. When Boise foundries could supply iron fronts for business buildings, Tom Davis equipped his Main Street store. This picture shows off the handsome brickwork on the second floor. The occasion for the gathering of girls in white was not recorded

While Julia bought her supplies by the box, pound, can, or yard, Ed bought his by hundred-pound sackfuls and hauled them forty-five miles from Boise to the Dorsey Ferry near Grand View. He paid the crossing fee, and rode on to the ranch. The men in camp ate plenty of rice, beans, bacon, ham, corn meal, lard, prunes, currants, graham flour, salt, wheat flour, coffee, sugar, and tea.[15]

The outfit set up a household, probably in the town of Bruneau, the furnishings for which are listed in Himrod's books for "two setts plates," a sugar bowl and creamer, coffee mill, butter dish, syrup mug, a sett of spoons, butcher knife, potato masher, can opener, tea stand, and cake lifter. Some hired cook would be using a new mop stick and broom, table linen and other kitchen goods.[16]

One day in September 1886, there was an accident at the Bar O. Someone sent an urgent appeal, delivered via the telegraph and Oregon Short Line Railroad, which ran east-west near Indian Creek, to Doctor Smith in Boise. He and Julia immediately started off for Bruneau. Particulars were unclear, but Ed McCrum had been hurt somehow by the fall of a horse.[17]

They found him still unconscious from the fall. It was branding time, and Ed had lassoed a calf. Upon checking his horse, it reared up and fell over backward, throwing him and injuring his head and spine. Julia and the doctor brought him to Lafayette Cartee's house on Grove Street. His family and many friends hoped for the best, but he died on September 24.[18]

The tragedy ended the "McCrum" name in the family cattle business, but the Bar O continued to operate. It was one of several outfits grazing thousands of cattle in the Bruneau country. Sheep arrived to compete in the 1880s, but the Bar O managed to survive this competition and several droughts. After harsh winters elsewhere in the late 1880s, Bruneau cattle were shipped to Montana and Wyoming. Eventually, the three sons of Tom and Julia would work at the Bruneau ranch—and at two other ranches their father developed.[19]

Cattle required winter feed. Tom had his eye on Government Island. The army relinquished its reserve in 1884, making it available to private ownership. A man named George Breidensteen purchased a large part of it and built an irrigating canal along the south edge of the property in 1886. This improvement made the property more productive.[20]

In 1888, Tom began assembling the various parcels of Government Island. By 1890 he had acquired the last piece, known as "the Purdom tract at the upper end," bringing his holding there to about 650 acres. Tom was in his mid-fifties and commanded enough wealth and labor to delegate both physical and managerial labors to others. Soon known as the GI Ranch, it supported hay and cattle. Tom leased the land at the upstream end to his Chinese associates, who grew large gardens of onions, strawberries, and other produce. They also raised hogs, for which they sent their wagon teams through the neighborhoods of Boise to collect garbage.[21]

Tom then took advantage of improvements affecting Long Valley north of Boise. Until the federal government began surveying this part of the Territory in 1880, few settlers had tried to overcome the winter snows and lack of a road. Boise leaders advocated that the army build a road to connect Fort Boise to Fort Lapwai. In 1882, when the Union Pacific was building the Oregon Short Line, it needed railroad ties. Contractors sent three hundred men to cut lumber, where they pruned forests all the way to the shore of Payette Lake. In the late 1880s, people who had taken herds from the Boise valley to graze in Round and Long valleys during the summer, finally began to homestead. The path between Boise and Long valleys gradually became more well-worn, and around 1898, Tom paid cash—as was his habit—for three homesteads at Van Wyck. He soon converted them to a buckaroo camp. The summer's work included managing the cattle and cutting, stacking, and storing wild hay, timothy and clover.[22]

With his characteristic willingness to innovate, Tom Davis decided to buy a few Hereford bulls. He had become aware of this English breed as it became more popular in the United States, perhaps had even seen a few issues of *Breeder's Journal,* an Illinois publication promoting the breed. A small group of breeders met in 1881 in Chicago to organize the American Hereford Association. At that time, only 200 head had entered the United States.[23]

Hereford. Tom Davis was for many years the only owner of Hereford cattle in Idaho. Experimenting with a new breed was entirely consistent with his progressive attitude to change and development.

The Swan Land and Cattle Company in Wyoming introduced Herefords to their breeding stock around 1878. John Sparks of Nevada tried them out as well. These stockmen learned that Herefords were tough. They could winter over on the northern states' plains, reducing wintering costs. They survived long drives from the range to the railroad. In addition, Herefords acquired their fat while young, making for highly marketable "baby beef." As a matter of economic profitability, the ratio at which they converted grass to flesh was very attractive.[24]

So Tom Davis bought Herefords, apparently the first rancher in Idaho to do so. John Sparks probably sold him a few, but the cowboys in southwest Idaho believed that Tom had "sent one of his boys to England to buy some bulls. He came back with several… and he had pretty good cattle." As they ranged in Long Valley or in the Boise foothills, the Herefords hardly needed branding, as their white faces, unique among all other breeds, were brand enough.[25]

Courtesy of Davis and McCrum family descendants

Thomas Jefferson Davis (1838-1908). Tom's highly diversified career included the raising and sale of vegetables, grain, hay, and fruit; the ranging of cattle at three ranches; operating a general store, including its freighting service; investments in banks, water and electric companies, and a brick factory; and a substantial Boise real estate enterprise. He and Julia gave riverfront land to Boise for a park.

— Chapter Eight —

LEADING CITIZEN

T he closest Tom Davis came to holding a political office was in 1864 when the "Union" party was seating delegates for a county convention at Centerville in the Boise Basin. The committee on credentials reported that Tom Davis was one of five people entitled to a seat representing Boise City. Tom and two of the others apparently weren't expected to be present, as a proxy was named to represent them.[1]

It isn't clear whether this appointment was a gesture of esteem by his fellow Unionist friends and associates or something he had sought. Hereafter, Tom Davis asserted leadership by virtue of his reputation for fair-minded practices in business, by expressing his views on public issues, and by contributing whatever assets he had useful to the civic enterprise at hand.

In June 1877, for example, Boise was considering two civic issues. A sculptor named Charles Ostner had given the Territorial Legislature a statue of George Washington in 1869. This statue was displayed in Boise's "public square," a block reserved for public buildings but, as yet, vacant. The statue needed repair, and the promoters of this improvement also wanted to fence the square. The "pass the hat" techniques of 1877 were similar to those still in use 125 years later. Citizens were asked to "subscribe" or pledge a certain amount of money to the cause, which often resulted in their names being published in the newspaper along with further appeals for more subscribers. To this effort, donations ranged between $1 to $20. Tom subscribed $10, one of about forty donations.[2]

The second issue was a school tax election. Members of the school board of trustees wanted to raise the property tax by three mills on the dollar in order to build an addition onto the existing school. The matter was controversial. Those opposed argued that the building was so decrepit that it should be abandoned for an altogether new building, a good and substantial building made of brick.

When the voters defeated the tax by only fifteen votes, two of the trustees expressed their disappointment by lashing out at "big taxpayers" like Tom Davis, who had, during the days before the election, made his views known. They interpreted his vote as a vote against public schools. He asserted once more that it was short-sighted to throw money onto a worthless building. If funds were needed merely to keep the school open until the end of the school year, he said he could collect the money easily from himself and others who had voted against the tax.[3]

Railroad issues took more time to conclude. When Boise learned that the Union Pacific and Central Pacific railroads would connect the two coasts of the country in 1869, citizens organized themselves to promote a connection between the transcontinental line and Portland, Oregon—a line that would pass through Boise. Boise's ambitions, however, were somewhat ahead of its economic power. The population was about 1,000 in 1869, not enough for the rail companies to consider a Boise rail connection an urgent priority.[4]

Little happened for another ten years. All of Boise grew tired of the long overland journey—with its weather problems, transfer costs, multi-day travel time, security issues—to the transcontinental rail head at Kelton. Business would be altogether better when Boise's people and products could travel faster and farther to reach distant markets.

Tom Davis was in the group of bankers and businessmen keeping an eye on national railroad developments. When the Oregon Short Line (OSL) at last was under construction to connect the Utah and Northern

Railroad in eastern Idaho to Huntington, Oregon, the group expected and hoped the line would enter Boise. However, Union Pacific decided not to undertake the expense of bringing this "main line" down—and perforce, back up—the grade of Ada County's many step-down benches to the elevation of the Boise River. Instead, the road followed Indian Creek, south of Boise. The railhead closest to Boise was a flat place in the desert that became known as Kuna. While the fourteen miles between Kuna and Boise was a vast improvement, not having a depot in town still was an expense and a nuisance—on muddy days, a four-hour nuisance. In 1883, the line went into operation to Huntington, Oregon, connecting to Portland.[5]

The Boise group adjusted its goals for a new target: a branch line connecting the new town of Nampa to Boise. They understood this would require undertaking some of the costs. The grade was no less of a problem than it had been before despite Boise's growing population, which had nearly doubled in ten years.

In this effort, Tom Davis' most pertinent asset was his land. After the disappointment of 1883, the Boise men determined to cultivate cordial relations with OSL representatives. More to the point, they pledged their personal funds, ranging between $100 and $5,000, to finance some of the preparatory work to get the railroad to Boise.[6]

In January 1884, the Boise subscribers met and, after discussions with the railroad representatives, agreed to preserve the right-of-way for the branch line and sell it to the railroad. They decided that the line would bridge the Boise River west of town and that the depot would be on the south side of Front Street between Ninth and Twelfth streets. Tom Davis cooperated with this plan, as he owned the depot site and a good part of the approach to it. They drew up a survey map, identified the centerline for the road, and became familiar with its "station number" mileage markers.[7]

Tom already had sold various parcels along the northern edge of his holdings. Several acres had gone to James Flanagan to expand his brickyard at the east edge of Boise, for example. Lafayette Cartee had bought some of Davis' land to enlarge his tree nursery and garden business.[8]

ISHS 2026

George Washington. Charles Ostner carved this statue and presented it to the Territorial Legislature in honor of Idaho pioneers. He painted a picture of its dedication day in Boise's public square. Tom Davis once donated towards the repair of the statue and a fence around the square.

On March 18, 1884, the OSL purchased from Tom Davis 100 feet of right-of-way, entering the west boundary of Davis' land, and another seventeen acres "in grounds" for the depot for a total cost of $8,000. For her part, as was customary when the common property of a married couple was to be sold, Julia Davis agreed before a witness to release all of her "right, title, interest in, or any dower" to the land.[9]

But the Union Pacific failed the city again in the spring of 1885 because of an "embarrassed" financial condition. If Boise leaders would build it, however, the railroad would turn over the right-of-way it had acquired. So the committee began figuring out how much money this would require: $40,000 for ties, $15,000 for the Boise River bridge, $10,000 for remaining right-of-way. All it took was for Boise businessmen to join the common effort and contribute "according to his means." So they continued.[10]

For Tom and other producers, railroad troubles also included shipping rates. The fruit growers, John Krall, Lafayette Cartee, himself, and others, were trying to compete for Montana and Colorado markets against growers in Utah and Washington. They found themselves at a competitive disadvantage because railroad rates were not proportionate to distances. At a meeting with railroad officials to discuss the problem, Tom's comments reveal that his basic outlook as a pioneer citizen had not diminished since the time he planted his first crops:

> *Mr. Davis showed in a very clear manner that if the railroad companies favored the fruit growers, such a course would do more to foster and build up the country than any other one thing.*[11]

"Building up the country" was the general mission of most self-conscious pioneers, and Tom Davis was still at it. The railroad men were not encouraging, but Davis and Krall made some headway with their requests for favorable rates on partial carloads.

Another "building up" project of Boise's business leaders was the organization of an electric light company in 1886. It was yet another case of "subscribers" putting up shares to finance some improvement, in this case the purchase of "dynamos" and the construction of a plant large enough to light the city. Among many others, Tom Davis subscribed for 25 shares at $10 a share. When the Boise City Electric Light Company was ready to incorporate, he served on its first board of directors.[12]

Unfortunately, various railroad setbacks delayed the entry of the branch line into Boise and to the reserved depot site. In 1887, a Boston investor helped finance a line from Nampa to Boise but couldn't afford to get the line down the last grade into town and across the river. Instead, the depot was about a mile south of Boise River near the edge of the "first" bench. Boiseans called this line "the Stub." The OSL finally managed—with the substantial aid, assets, and energies of Boise businessmen—to bring its line into town in 1893. The new passenger depot was completed in 1895 at Tenth and Front streets, exactly where Tom Davis and the other faithful subscribers had planned it for so long.[13]

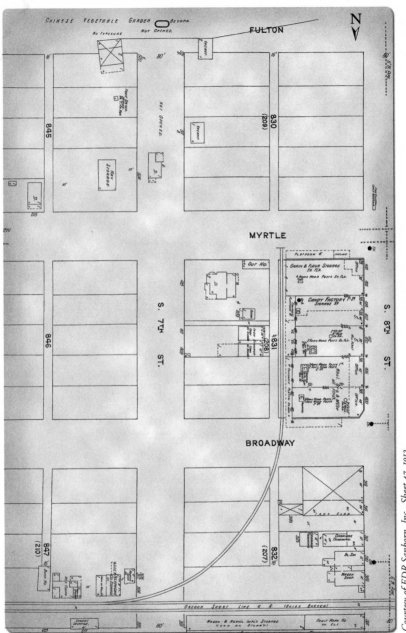

Courtesy of EDR Sanborn, Inc., Sheet 47, 1912.

Davis house location. Built in 1889, the family's second house occupied the corner now known as Capitol Boulevard and Myrtle Street. Their first home was probably closer to the river. This 1912 view shows Davis' fruit dryer, hay and apple storage buildings, and other utility buildings then vacant. Chinese vegetable gardens are at south edge of map.

The Davis House, 1891. The entry steps faced the lane to the east, which later became Seventh Street and then Capitol Boulevard. The first floor included drawing, dining, and library rooms, and a hallway for a "broad stairway." The young man posing in front is unidentified.

Tom Davis was ready for it. The last two years of the 1880s was a time of growth for the Davis family and for Boise in general. Tom and Julia had their sixth and last child, Hazel, in June of 1888. All four of the older children were still at home. Tommy, the eldest, was only thirteen years old. Clearly, it was a good time to build a bigger house.

The new Davis child was emblematic of how the entire town was growing. Times were prosperous. Boise was big enough to support such businesses as foundries, for example. Tom was an early customer and in 1889 put an iron front on his rental building on Main Street. The Territorial Legislature prepared for a convention to take place in Boise during the summer of 1889 to draw up a constitution, a prerequisite for statehood. Boise's leading citizens planned to make a good impression on the many visitors who would be in town during this important event. They fussed about how they might de-emphasize such negatives as brothels and dirty alleys. They saw to it that convention guests be taken on carriage rides to tour more edifying attractions such as the valley's better farms and Tom Davis' orchard.[14]

Tom and Julia hired Alex McPherson, a contractor and builder to build a wood frame house not far from the one they would abandon. Tom and Julia expected McPherson to complete the house quickly. It was to have two and a half stories, modern conveniences, and a hot air furnace. Not counting halls, bathrooms, and closets, it would have nine "principle rooms." Nearby, Tom and Julia also had begun a far more grand house, a "larger mansion" that would take more time to complete. By the end of September, the builder had dug its basement, lined it with cut stone, and dressed it "in the best style."[15]

In his typical way, Tom Davis had not advertised his personal business. But a newspaper reporter got wind of the new house and asked Davis more about it. He learned that Tom and Julia had surveyed parts of their property and were getting ready to subdivide. This was welcome news to the reporter, who headlined his article about Tom's plans, "More room; more houses."[16]

In 1890 Tom, nursing 30,000 new prune trees and still in the midst of an apple business so large he was shipping apples to Montana by full carloads, created two city "additions" in response to the pressure of growth and his expectation that a depot would end up on Front Street. He recorded the first one in May. His plan continued the original grid of the city southward, extending the north-south streets in conformity to the original plat. His new house would be roughly on the line of Seventh Street (later named Capitol Boulevard). Until this time, access to the Davis residence had been the Davis' private lane.[17]

The plat of Davis' (First) Addition brought Eighth and Ninth streets south past Front Street as well, and provided extra width on Front Street. The three blocks and their lots were arranged with the alley running north-south. Rail trackage would run between the freight depot and the warehouse businesses that would flourish there. The new east-west streets were Broadway (later renamed Broad), Myrtle, and Fulton.[18]

The other plat, Central Subdivision, lay east of Fifth Street and south of Front Street. This area was in demand for residences. The east-west streets lined up with Broad and Myrtle streets, although Tom waited until 1906 to subdivide the land between Fifth and Eighth streets.[19]

Tom and Julia sold the first lot in the Davis Addition in July of 1890. For $2,000, John Bennett bought two whole lots and fifteen feet of a third (for 65 feet of frontage) on the east side of Ninth Street. Tom must have appreciated the cash, as this was the summer he purchased 93 acres of Government Island from John and Martha Gakey, for which he had to pay $7,000.[20]

Demand for sales and leases was strong enough to continue the business lots from Fulton Street all the way to the river in a "second" Davis addition creating Battery and Water streets. Ninth Street was a busy one, as it was the path to the old bridge over the Boise River, the Ninth Street Pike, also known in these days, however ruefully, as the "road to Kuna."[21]

Thus, Tom recycled portions of his land from its multiple agricultural uses to real estate sales and leases, both business and residential. The development contributed substantially to the family's wealth, thanks largely to Tom's fortuitous choice of land directly between a future townsite and the river and a willingness to adapt and change.

With each new street, new alley, and new building, a few more rows of Tom Davis' apple trees disappeared. By now, some of them were twenty-five years old and of substantial size. The environs immediately surrounding the lawn of Davis' new house would contain orchard trees for a while longer, but the reporter said that the original Davis house would "disappear from the scene" as soon as the family moved to its new quarters.[22]

The reporter excused his intrusion into Tom Davis' family affairs by saying, "the point isn't so much the Davis' new house, but the fact that Boise's cry for more room and more houses has made the apple trees quake in their tap roots and prepare to give way for something more needed" — namely, blocks and lots to allow for more people to live in Boise.[23]

While Tom and Julia were in the midst of replacing trees with city lots, they learned that Frank Davis died suddenly on March 8, 1891. He had cancer but his death was unexpected when it happened. Frank had become associated with the Methodist church, at which a large attendance gathered for his last rites and the procession to the cemetery. The newspaper obituary said little else, noting that he had "accumulated a comfortable fortune" and was held "in high esteem by all who knew him." Hester took charge of their interest in a band of sheep and continued to manage the dairy for a number of years. She began subdividing their land in 1908, creating Pleasanton Addition, Frank Davis Addition, and Hester Davis Subdivision.[24]

Growth was warmly welcomed by a community optimistic for the better things bound to result from a larger population, statehood, and prospering businesses. One hundred new dwellings were built in 1890, all of which were immediately "packed" and fully occupied, every available room rented. The population increased by 25 percent in one year. In 1891, the building inventory increased by 220 buildings. The next few years brought the city ever more assets, among them a sewer system, the new Columbia Theater (reputed to be the largest public hall between the Missouri River and the West Coast), a new City Hall, an electric light plant, an electric street railroad, and a new hospital.[25]

In the end, Tom and Julia abandoned their idea for a commodious mansion. The family remained among the apple trees in the "temporary" house, which apparently had room enough for five growing children and style enough for their practical parents.

Chapter Nine

JULIA GOES TO THE FAIR

A s their children matured, Tom and Julia gave them as many advantages as they could. Some observers felt that Tom was "indulgent to the extreme" with his children and that Julia tried to impose discipline not altogether successfully. After losing Marion, discipline might have been a difficult skill for these parents to practice convincingly. One story about discipline (of a sort) was told by the principal of Boise High School, where Tom, Jr., was in his senior year. The story may say more about a child so relaxed about potential consequences that he found it easy to play hookey from school.[1]

Tom the father came to the school one "glorious October morning" to convey some message to his son. Upon learning that Tommy was not at school, he appeared surprised but said little and left. The next Sunday evening, someone knocked at the back door of the principal's home, tossed in a neatly wrapped package containing a loin quarter of venison, and left quickly. The principal guessed who it was and noticed the next day at school how Tom "smiled and twinkled." In this way, Tom avoided any serious punishment for his deer-hunting truancy.[2]

Tommy was the only Davis child to attend Boise High. Etta and Hazel attended St. Margaret's Academy, a school for girls associated with St. Michael's Episcopal Church, of which the Davis family were active members. Edwin went to Philips Exeter Academy in New Hampshire and then spent some time at the University of Notre Dame in Indiana.[3]

Despite their parents' wealth and devotion to education, the children were not always receptive to parental prescriptions. Harry was reported variously located on the Bruneau or at one of the other Bar O cow camps while he was of an age to be at school, although he and Thomas were reported on their way to Oberlin, Ohio, to enter college in December of 1893. Harry would die at age 32 in 1910. The death notice in the newspaper said he had been suffering from heart trouble for the year previous. Years later, Long Valley cowboys who had known the Davis boys recalled that they "drank a little several times more than they needed to."[4]

In his last year at Exeter, Edwin "skipped to England on a cattle boat" without parental leave. His hopes to join a big band and travel the world as a musician had not materialized by the time his money ran low. He dared to cable his father for more. As frantic as they were angry, Tom and Julia sent him only enough for his return ticket to Boise. Knowing he had work to do to return to his mother's good graces, he used some of his funds to buy her a bottle of costly perfume in an attractive bottle and then set sail for home. Julia treasured the gift until her death.[5]

Like many other women in Boise, Julia was involved in charitable work through her church and participated in *ad hoc* calls to raise funds for various community causes. In 1892 she responded to a call from two of her friends who had acquired responsibilities in the promotion of the World's Columbian Exposition, to be held at Chicago and so named to commemorate the 400th anniversary of Columbus' discovery of America.

The fair authorities in Chicago had made Bertha Palmer, wife of hotel-builder Potter Palmer, the chair of the Women's Board of Lady Managers. When Mrs. Palmer asked each state to appoint a woman to serve on this board, Idaho Governor Norman Willey appointed Alice Straughn, the wife of Idaho's Surveyor General. In her turn, Alice appointed a woman in each Idaho county to form "Columbian Clubs" and create interest among Idahoans for the fair. In Ada County, she appointed Carrie Logan, whose husband was serving at the time on the Ada County Board of County Commissioners.[6]

Meanwhile, the Idaho State Legislature, particularly sensitive to its recent elevation to Statehood in 1890, determined to support an Idaho presence at the fair. It appropriated $50,000 to construct an Idaho Building to help advertise the state and its rich timber, mineral, and horticultural resources. The two-story building, designed by Cutter and Poetz of Spokane, was a rustic chalet-like structure made of logs. The first floor featured a fireplace, offices, sleeping apartments for the staff, and toilet rooms. The second floor was the Women's Reception Room, a place where visitors could rest and refresh themselves. The architects intended this room to recall a miner's cabin. However, the legislature provided no funds for furnishing the interior.[7]

Alice Straughn and Carrie Logan called the women of Ada County together at a mass meeting on May 2, 1892. Julia Davis and about forty other mostly well-to-do women gathered at the Statehouse in the House of Representatives. They elected officers — Victoria Louise Eoff, president; Mary Hallock Foote, vice-president — and determined that the object of the group would be to furnish and care for the Women's Reception Room. The names of the women attending the meeting were placed in a box and then drawn at random to create eight groups, which would raise as much money as possible, but no less than $25 each, in whatever way appealed.

Records weren't kept of who was in each group or how each earned its quota. One group sold cottage cheese made by one of its members. Another held a promenade concert on the grounds of the Capitol building, for which they closed all of the iron gates in the fence surrounding the block except for the one on Jefferson Street and charged 25 cents for admission. Boise's brass band dressed in their uniforms and played the concert. This committee brought in $149. As late as April 1893, the women were still fundraising. They sponsored a dance at the Natatorium, an indoor thermal-water swimming pool at the eastern edge of town which had a cover for dances and other party occasions. This event was intended to appeal to Boise's younger crowd. For this evening, street cars ran every fifteen minutes beginning at 7:30 p.m.; music began at 8:30 p.m.; dancing, at 9 p.m. Guests had dinner at one of eight tables, each decorated in a different color, hosted by one of the club members and her husband, one of them Tom and Julia Davis. The evening netted the club $63.60.[8]

During that spring of 1893, much else besides the fair occupied Boise citizens. The new five-story City Hall building neared completion in April. Tom Davis and the others working to bring the Union Pacific railroad into town were about to realize their plans. They were dealing with last-minute right-of-way problems and transforming their interests to a new company they called the Boise Railway and Terminal Company. In cooperation with Union Pacific, they were building the line into the city, the depot, and its associated freight houses. Builders were hauling stone onto the depot site on Front Street. All hoped to erect the railroad bridge across the river before the spring snow-melt brought its usual flood down Boise River.[9]

Tom Davis had begun to diversify his stock business. Aside from selling cattle, he was now advertising "Driving and Draft Horses for sale by Thomas Davis, Boise." His logo was the profile of an elegant horse and carriage in black silhouette. His fruit enterprise was focused more on volume sales than winning prizes. In all of the discussions of Idaho's horticultural exhibits, and how the prized fruit was chemically preserved in glass jars for its sojourn and stay in Chicago, and how Idaho's display of peaches, pears, apples, grapes, and plums was "the wonder of all who see it," and how the exhibit was a major compliment to Idaho, Tom was not identified as one of the contributors.[10]

Boise's newspaper in 1893 supplies a glimpse of the settings in which Boise's influential women networked and discussed their projects and their next moves. In mid-April, for example, Mrs. George H. Steward held an "at-home," attended by fifty-seven women, including Julia Davis. Someone poured coffee and chocolate. The women enjoyed table service while an orchestra, stationed upstairs, "discoursed sweet music all afternoon." The women discussed their social and other business amidst a "floral garniture" of carnations, pansies, roses, and smilax while streamers of pink and green ribbon decorated "with charming effect." Two weeks later, Julia was one of fifty women who attended another at-home hosted by Della Himrod.[11]

Julia McCrum Davis was a charter member of the Columbian Club of Boise.

Contributions for the Women's Reception Room accumulated. The governor offered his piano. Mary Foote designed a settee, table, and chairs to be made of solid oak, the lot to be built in Chicago. One of the women embroidered the linens for the table and a sideboard. Others donated china and rugs. Some of the funds they raised provided a salary of $40 per month for a woman to supervise the room and serve refreshments and hospitality to its visitors.[12]

Throughout the first months of 1893, the fair's promotional efforts were evident in Idaho. The *Statesman* published articles and news of the fair almost daily. As opening day on May 1 approached, the paper was full of descriptions of exhibits and buildings under construction and promised attractions. Advertisers were selling accident insurance. Railroads described their rates—a thousand trains were expected to enter or leave Chicago every day. People were demanding through train service because "It is old-fashioned to change cars." Idaho's fair commissioner James M. Wells filed frequent reports about the progress of Idaho's exhibits of minerals, fruits, angora, and other commodities. In early March, he said that the state seal was ready to ship in forty pieces, to be assembled and mounted above the entrance to the Idaho Building. In April, he was trying to put together an exhibit of Idaho opal from the Snake River area near Hot Springs Ferry.[13]

The fair did open on May 1 despite the fact that it was not fully complete. Alice Straughn and two other Boise women attended the opening but the general advice was that Idaho people should wait until after June 1 to attend, when more attractions would be operating. Detailed reports described how to get to the fair ground, which was located east of Chicago in a one-mile square park on the shore of Lake Michigan, by taking an eight-car train which ran every three minutes. During the next weeks, information poured out of Chicago about hotel prices, fares, what else to see in Chicago, how to remain safe, how to economize, where to eat. From Boise to Chicago and return, the fare was $88.50.[14]

"A great many are talking of and getting ready to go," reported the newspaper, mentioning Mrs. Eoff and Mrs. Ridenbaugh. Women's afternoon socials continued to supply the venues for such talk. Julia attended a musicale at a friend's home the first week of May. They might also have discussed the progress of a free kindergarten for poor children that the "ladies" of Boise were organizing. Boise had children so poor that they didn't know what ice cream was, and the ladies were, among other things, introducing them to it. Members of the Boise Relief Society were also active, providing "organized relief, intelligently directed," for food, fuel, medicine and other needs of the sick and destitute.[15]

In the Davis household, fair business was intertwined with young Tom's imminent graduation from Boise High School. Towards the end of May, graduation exercises were in the planning stages. Thomas Jefferson Davis was one of the few students who had begun his education in Boise's primary schools and continued to the senior year.[16]

Tom, and no doubt his family, were fully engulfed in graduation rituals. His class went on the traditional picnic, a subsidiary purpose of which was to collect evergreen boughs for decorating the stage of the Columbia Theater, where the ceremonies would take place. This was the second year of the DeLamar Contest, a declamatory competition established by the wealthy miner and entrepreneur, J.R. DeLamar. His fund allowed for striking the winners' medals. Miss Branstetter's medal from the 1892 competition was on display at Doty's jewelry store on Eighth Street.

Tom was rehearsed and ready. Parents, siblings, and friends dressed their best and filled the parquet, dress circle, and gallery of the theater. After musical selections by the Philharmonic Orchestra, the students performed their pieces. Tom recited "The Chariot Race," from the novel *Ben Hur* by Lew Wallace. The large audience appreciated his "spirited and thrilling" rendition, but first prize went to Hattie Himrod and second to Edgar Thomas Hawley. Mayor James Pinney presented the medals.[17]

The next evening was commencement, the 8th annual for the school. The stage was "intensely decorated" with the students' evergreens, flowers, and borrowed house plants, many in full bloom. Upon an easel near the back, a poster said, "He Conquers Who Endures." The orchestra played an overture. The nine graduates marched to the stage and joined Governor McConnell, the Reverend J.C. Gallaudet, and their principal, C.M. Higgins. Someone gave the class history and prophecy for the future. Each student delivered an oration and was handed a bundle of flowers from admiring friends by small girls dressed in white. Tom's oration about "Reserve Powers" was well reviewed as "full of vim and energy." The students sang their class song. After a short speech from Governor McConnell, they received their diplomas and a benediction by Reverend Gallaudet.[18]

School affairs weren't over for the Davis family. Etta, still in the primary grades, was involved in the closing exercises at St. Margaret's. She had been rehearsing a duet dance with her friend, Ermina Heyburn, a piano solo, and another number called "La Recreation Perdue." These were performed in one of the classrooms, decorated for the occasion in yellow and white.[19]

As soon as these rituals ended, Julia Davis—and many other mothers and children—packed to go to the fair. Julia was taking Tom, most likely a graduation gift. On a fresh morning in early June, the two boarded the Chicago-bound train along with Mrs. Eastman, Mrs. Regan, and several of their lucky children.[20]

World's Columbian Exposition at Chicago, 1893 (for the railroad trade) courtesy of Mark Baltes

World's Columbian Exposition. The exposition grounds integrated canals, lagoons, grand walkways, views, and gardens amidst the buildings and other fair attractions. The Women's Building, enlarged right, contained a model hospital, kindergarten, and kitchen. Its exhibits featured the "philanthropic, charitable, and reformatory work of women all over the globe."

The husbands remained in Boise, probably because railroad affairs demanded their full attention just at that moment. The laying of the rails into town was to begin on June 12. The elder Davis attended the fair later in June, stopping in Denver on his way home to obtain the latest information on the fruit market in Colorado. He reported that "trade was depressed" and would offer little demand for Idaho fruit. The United States had entered into a financial panic early in May, contributing to the disappointing results in the fruit trade. However, it did nothing to suppress the ability of Boise's wealthy citizens to attend the fair.[21]

Once in Chicago, Julia and Tom, Jr., wasted no time making their way from the busy center of Chicago to the "White City," so called because the fair's exhibit halls and buildings were mostly white, well coordinated as to

ISHS 80-2.88/b

The Idaho Building. Women-power made up for the omission of official funding for the interior of Idaho's state building at the fair. The log building showed Idaho's forest resources to good advantage and was a gathering place for Idaho visitors.

height and proportion, and surrounded by gardens, pools, pleasant walks, and lovely views. Landscapes had been designed by Henry Law Olmstead, and by June, the plantings were producing his desired soothing and evocative effect. The fair had clean public bathrooms, pure water, ambulance service, a sewage processing system, and day care for children. The fair's square mile of loveliness and order was a potent contrast to the city of Chicago, which was grimy, dark, noisy, polluted, and not particularly safe.[22]

Julia and Tom went to the Idaho Building and signed the guest register, the same day that Idaho Senator George L. Shoup was there. They were greeted in the Women's Reception Room. Julia could see that the cedar logs and wooden floor had been attractively stained and decorated with the donated rag rugs. The heavy oak table, chairs, and rockers looked well, probably not much like a miner's cabin furnishings. A lava-rock fireplace was in a deep recess along one wall, and on each side of it were five shelves for books and other items. A balcony surrounded the entire floor, so visitors could stroll about and obtain a view of the fair in all directions.[23]

Julia and every other Columbian Club woman who visited the room visited her own accomplishment, the product of her own labor, organizational skills, and pride as a woman. The exposition also had a Women's Building designed by a female architect. Its exhibits, all designed by women, covered topics such as medicine, hygiene, education, and a multitude of other subjects. A Women's Congress considered issues of suffrage and child care. The "sphere" of women's potential influence obviously was moving well beyond a woman's home and hearth.[24]

The Boise newspaper continued to list the Idaho visitors who signed the register at the fair and, when the reporters could obtain them, the rest of the fairgoers' itineraries. Most had additional destinations, visiting relatives and friends in the East, and collecting students attending boarding schools. Men like Tom Davis combined the trip with business. Julia's widowed mother was still living in Galt and may well have received a visit from her daughter and grandson.

The Boise women who had raised the money for their small corner of the fair—along with countless others among the fair's 27 million visitors—returned home and continued talking about what they had seen. Cities, it seemed, might be places of beauty and social harmony. They did not have to be dark and dirty. The fair ended on October 31, 1893, but Columbian Club women still had fair-related business. The oak table and chairs were shipped to Boise. The women determined to create a public reading room and library on the thus-far unused third floor of the new Boise City Hall. The furnishings would go there. They decided to continue the Columbian Club for this new object.[25]

The call went out. Julia and the others responded, fully charged by their previous success and optimism for new work. The club re-organized in October 1894 under the same name. Their constitution said they would undertake work to "promote the highest interests of the city." They sorted themselves into committees and got busy once more. One committee was called "Town and Village Improvement." The contrast between the White and Black cities of Chicago had given rise to a movement to beautify and soften cities all over the United States, and the Columbian Club had carried its flag into Boise.

- *Chapter Ten* -

THE PARK

In the years after the fair and until her death, Julia Davis continued paying her Columbian Club dues of $1, gave larger sums when "subscriptions" were collected for causes, and took her turn on various committees. The reading room at City Hall, which was staffed in the beginning by the women themselves as volunteers, proved to be the seed for the Boise Public Library, a traveling library for Idaho's rural residents, and the Idaho State Library.[1]

The club's impulse for civic improvement quickly turned to the city's trees, public spaces, and parks. The women persuaded the Boise City Council to pass a law prohibiting the destruction and mutilation of shade trees by those stringing up telephone and electric light wires. Then they let the Ada County Board of County Commissioners know that the ground surrounding the courthouse was "in great need" of shade trees. All the women really needed was permission to plant trees themselves, which they did.[2]

The years between 1898-1900 were full of talk in Boise about public parks. Advocacy for parks wasn't new. An effort in 1890 to get the city to purchase the 150-acre fair grounds for $15,000 had failed. In 1893, Mayor James Pinney had suggested publicly that Boise create a park but with no results. Expense to taxpayers was a major barrier.[3]

Music Box. Tom Davis wound up this music box each evening as the family sat down for supper.

In these two years, Gertrude Hays was president of the Columbian Club. The Improvement Committee tried to persuade the Boise City Council to establish a real public park. They identified possible alternative locations, then invited and accompanied members of the council to inspect them. One site was a forty-acre parcel of land on the north side of Boise River owned by Tom and Julia Davis.[4]

Julia's husband, obviously part of the club's behind-the-scenes network and probably looking for the best moment to make a move in concert with the club's agitation, wrote a letter to the city council in September 1899. He offered to give the Davis' river-front land to the city. The city council minutes for September 7 say:

> *A communication was read from Mr. Thomas Davis relative to a location for a City Park provided the city comply with certain conditions. On motion, the communication was referred to Committee on Flumes and Gulches together with the Mayor, City Engineer, and Attorney.[5]*

Tom's letter has not survived. The "conditions" probably related to flood-control problems with low-lying ground close to the river. Whether the committee made its report off-record, or whether it dropped the idea because of more pressing business is not known. No further reference is found in city council minutes. Tom and Julia held onto the land. The oral tradition in the Davis family is that Tom reminded the city council of the offer more than once in the next few years.

As the century turned, the Davis family carried on much as it had before. Upon sitting down to dinner every night, Tom Davis wound up the German music box that rested on the mantel. He continued indulging his children. In 1900 Etta wrote to Edwin at Notre Dame, "I guess dear little Hazel has been made a great deal over this winter. She wrote that father had a saddle made for her." She also had a pet deer in a fenced enclosure behind the house.[6] Julia wrote newsy letters to her children while they were away at school, To "My dear Edd" at Notre Dame, she wrote:

We received your letter some days ago and sorry to have been so long in writing, but have been so busy trying to have the house in order before Etta [who had been visiting Galt] returned... Harry came in from the cow camp Friday night, left Monday with Hutchinson. He was going to the camp and bring in some old cows... We had a nice little Jersey cow—we found her dead Monday morning. She bloated. Mr. Joy the druggist buried his little girl yesterday. Pneumonia and whooping cough. She was 6 years.

Your father says you can have a clarinet. You should. I think you should correspond with some musical stores and find out where you could do the best, and on the way home get it. The Boys band is improving. They play twice a week... Perkins is still their leader.

I hope you will not forget to thank your father. He sends you a draft of $10 No. 16575. We had quite a storm wind and rain Wednesday morning. Did a great deal of damage in Weiser. We are going to have a large fruit crop—cherries are quite large. The lawn looks well. We have a Swede, and he takes quite an interest in the yard. Lots of pansies in bloom. McCrums have a new clerk from Iowa. They have had their house painted light green dark green trimmings. It looks well.

I hope you are feeling well and learning fast and will come home a nice smart boy. You will find $10 in case [you] find out what you can buy a clarinet for. And let me know and if I think I can afford to buy it will write immediately.

Mother[7]

Despite the family's wealth, it appeared that Tom and Julia's children had no such thing as automatic access to it. In a letter Etta had written to Edwin from Galt a few weeks earlier, she said, "I am expecting father to send me money every day and will start for home any time after it comes."[8]

Tom Davis was busy with business in Boise. He served on the board of directors for the Bank of Commerce. He served a term as treasurer of the Electric Power Company, Ltd., and installed electric lights at the house. He invested in the Idaho Vitrified Brick and Pipe Company, which was located on or near his own property at the north end of Thirteenth Street. He owned shares in the Boise National Bank. Each year, one or more of the institutions with which he was associated contributed an ad to the Boise High School yearbook.[9]

At Government Island Ranch, Tom conducted spring cattle deals. One day in June 1900, for example, he entertained several buyers as they looked over 200 fat steers. One of the hired men, George Anderson, observed that "Mr. Davis gives but little encouragement. I hardly think he will make a contract early like last year."[10]

Julia's wide circle of friendship included women of varying degrees of intimacy. Aside from the Columbian Club, which certainly included close friends, she also entertained at home, a reciprocating obligation of all active women in her economic strata and a way of keeping information flowing. George Anderson wrote to Edwin, "Today your Mama and Mrs. Richardson gave an elaborate party to their lady friends in the city and you can rest assured I had to move around pretty briskly from morn till late evening." She also surrounded herself with a much smaller group that called themselves "the Monday Afternoon Club."[11]

Etta, aged twenty-two, was the first of the Davis children to marry. The wedding at the house in the summer of 1901 probably stressed not only Mr. Anderson, but a substantial cadre of other helpers and assistants. Bishop Funsten performed the evening ceremony at the lavishly decorated house. "Dear little Hazel" and her cousin LaVerne McCrum scattered sweet pea blossoms in the path of the bride. Etta, on the arm of her father, descended the broad stairway from the second floor into the drawing room. Julia wore a gown of "silk grenadine over taffeta with yoke of jetted net over cloth of silver." Tom's gift to his daughter was a "substantial check." The rooms were "resplendent with incandescent globes." Dinner followed, with the bride's table in the dining room and other tables scattered in the library. The guests danced and played games until 3 a.m., when they escorted Mr. and Mrs. William Quinn to the train depot. The couple headed for a honeymoon summer in Atlantic resorts and the Adirondack Mountains, then to New York City, where Quinn was in the book publishing business.[12]

In 1907 Edwin was in the midst of a troubled romance with Marcella Torrance, the daughter of one of Boise's foundry owners. He loved her, but she wasn't sure of her own feelings. That summer, Julia became ill enough to be confined in bed. When Marcella visited her one day, Julia confided that she didn't think she would live very much longer. She hoped Marcella would marry Edwin before she died.[13]

Julia died at home on September 19, 1907, at the age of sixty and before the couple married (on December 31, 1907). The newspaper said she had suffered from an ulcerated bowel for ten weeks. The funeral awaited Etta Davis Quinn's arrival from New York, and then her casket was covered with flowers from the Columbian Club, her daughters, and the women of the Episcopal church, in which she had been so active. The Monday Afternoon Club sent a floral arrangement in the shape of a broken wheel. Tom Davis' Elks Lodge associates sent their floral tribute to this "highly respected pioneer." She was buried at the Masonic Cemetery.[14]

Tom, who had executed the deed granting the forty acres to the city council for a park in February before Julia became ill, was at last able to

Courtesy of Davis and McCrum family descendants

Julia McCrum Davis (1847-1907). Julia was never intimidated by long-distance travel across the country, managed a substantial household, aided exhausted travelers arriving in Boise on the Emigrant Road, surrounded herself with gardens, "subscribed" to charitable causes, and collaborated with her husband to give Boise land for a park.

see the conclusion of the transaction. On November 22, 1907, the Boise City Council accepted the land for $1, this time with Tom's condition that it "always and forever be known as the Julia Davis Park."[15]

A few months before Julia's death, the Music Committee of the Columbia Club had undertaken to bring to Boise the largest musical program it had ever seen. They signed a contract with Walter Damrosch of New York, a former conductor of the New York Philharmonic Orchestra and then the conductor of his own sixty-piece orchestra. He would also bring an esteemed oratorio singer named Mary De Moss. They planned the performance for June 9, 1908. Damrosch required a guarantee of $2,000, which the Club expected to realize from ticket sales.

After they signed the contract, they learned that the Pinney Theater, which was under construction after the old Columbia Theater had been torn down, would not be completed by the date of the concert. The dismayed women consulted an attorney about how they might escape the contract, but were advised to go through with it or be liable for damages. The Riverside Pavilion west of Ninth Street, an open-air venue that had, at least, the virtue of bench seating, was available. The women decided they had no choice, reserved the date, marked the benches with seat numbers, and "prayed it wouldn't rain." They abandoned any thought of profiting from the concert and calculated prices to sell out and bring in the $2,000. They asked the railroad to provide special rates and schedules for people coming from neighboring counties, which it did. In downtown Boise, tickets went on sale at Ballou-Latimer's drug store on Eighth Street, where the seating "plat" was in the front window.[16]

Tom, consistent with a lifelong love of music he had shared with Julia during their thirty-six years together and his sympathy with Julia's enterprise in civic improvement, had encouraged the women to bring Damrosch to Boise. Naturally, he bought a ticket for the concert.[17]

Around the end of May, he acquired a bad cold involving a choking in his throat, which worried him. Still somewhat afflicted as the evening of the concert arrived, he was determined to attend. The weather was "perfect." The orchestra played, among other pieces, "Hungarian Rhapsody" by Franz Liszt. Miss De Moss delivered in fine voice. Damrosch proved to be a gracious guest, saying that performing in the open air was a novel experience for the orchestra—and in an exquisite setting.[18]

Tom enjoyed himself, greeting friends and expressing his pleasure that the concert had sold out. The Club made its $2,000 guarantee, and if President Mrs. McCalla had known it this evening, she might have whispered in his ear that they had exactly 50 cents and a 2-cent stamp left over.

Tom went home. The next morning, he did not appear for breakfast. The housekeeper found him as if asleep, but dead in his bed.[19]

The entire city paid attention while this pioneer was laid to rest next to Julia. The services began at his house under the management of Tom's Elks' Lodge, from whose ranks more than a hundred members attended, the largest such turnout in its history. His friends and colleagues were so numerous that two sets of pallbearers were named, the Honorary and the Active, among them Charles Himrod, Frank Coffin, and Tim Regan. After the cortege had arrived at the cemetery, and after the Elks members had heaped bouquets of flowers on the coffin, and after a male quartet sang "Nearer My God To Thee," and after the Elks members sang "The Vacant Chair," four Chinese men, still renting land from Tom Davis, advanced to the side of the grave. Each, hat in hand, bowed low and as near to the ground as possible. In accordance with Chinese burial custom, each held his hat momentarily and finally over the grave.[20]

— *Afterword* —

In his hand-written will, Tom Davis expressed his wish that his youngest son, Edwin, administer his estate. He bequeathed the ranches and cattle lands to his sons, the orchard property in Crane Creek to his daughters. He wanted all of these properties to continue intact in his name without being sold for at least ten years, earning income and rents in the meantime.

The probate court determined that the will was invalid for technical reasons, but the children knew their father's intent. When Edwin inventoried the estate, the children found themselves with over 2,100 acres of land, cattle, horses, bank stock, an insurance policy, cash, and the house, its furnishings, and Tom and Julia's personal property. They could expect a monthly income from the Davis Building on Main Street, other business rents, and the Chinese garden rents. Income could be realized from the sale of a few unsold lots in the Davis subdivisions. The stage was set for the second generation to write the story of its progress.

There were critics of the park gift. One hundred years later, it appears that they were merely without the vision to see above the boggy areas. Indeed, some of the land was low and subject to flooding. Within a couple of years after the gift had been accepted, the city invited the public to bring fill for the low ground, a practice also responsible for making the park resemble a "dump" at times. The Columbian Club planted trees and shrubs; Mayor W.E. Pierce planted a Kentucky Coffee Bean tree. Soon there was a playground, a band shell, grading plans, a lagoon, boat rentals, a zoo, and rules of deportment in the park: No advertising. No conduct of business. No preaching, praying, orating, or playing music without the permission of the city.

The gift of Julia Davis Park was an act of civic philanthropy, motivated by people who had long seen themselves as pioneers in building a city and who were simply continuing the project. It's hard to say that it was the "first" such act, but Boise had not seen the like of it before.

Considering the progress of Tom and Julia Davis in Boise, building a city requires of its citizens a willingness to live in the place for a long time, and to plunge a spade into whatever ground presents its promise. It requires people who know their talents and potential, who have the confidence to take a risk, and who understand that the risk can return its reward as slowly as an apple tree grows.

It requires faith that the future will be better than the past. A tent will be better than nothing. A log cabin will be more permanent than a tent. Brick will be more permanent than wood. When a town begins with nothing, it is obvious that new people will bring fresh resources, fresh energy, and a certain welcome weight to support new services, better hospitals, school teachers, ministers, librarians.

It requires a willingness both to lead and to follow, to join someone else's committee or to start one's own, and then to take turns filling chairs as board member, secretary, treasurer, president. It requires investment, putting one's money at risk and endlessly "subscribing" to the many enterprises that make a good place better: a railroad, an electric company, a brick factory, a bank, social justice, a school building, a chess club, a musical evening.

It requires a clear-eyed appreciation of what one has to offer the common good: an idea, money, land, labor, a pasture, tolerance for racial diversity, an opinion on a bond issue.

Tom and Julia Davis and their generation built Boise. It now requires later generations to believe that the day of pioneering cities is not over. A hundred years later, new ground lies waiting for a spade, an idea, a committee, a subscription... It is up to us to believe that Tom and Julia Davis were not the last of their kind.

Sarah Tregay photo

~ Acknowledgements ~

I wish to acknowledge and thank Patricia Hughes of Boise for the superb research she performed to discover the childhood facts about Tom and Frank Davis. Her alliance with a genealogical researcher named Ethel Trego of Monmouth, Illinois, yielded documents about the Davis brothers' birth parents and the Claycomb family: probate records, the bonding order, census data, obituaries, and other materials. Her wonderful bundle landed in my lap, a rare gift.

Thanks to those who read portions of the manuscript where the topic was one of their specialties: Mark Baltes on the Davis house location, Ann Felton on railroad and depot matters, and Leslie Frazho on the McCrum family. Ann, while serving as Boise City Historian, found and shared a revealing box of 1920s and 1930s records pertaining to Julia Davis Park. Mark contributed one of the illustrations of the Columbia World's Fair.

Thanks to Arthur Hart, who telephoned one morning to give me a list of several *Statesman* clippings about Tom Davis that he had gathered over the years.

Thanks to the remarkable community of historians, librarians, archivists, and curators who work at the Idaho History Center, Idaho State Historical Museum, Boise State University's Special Collections Library, and Boise

Public Library: especially Kathy Hodges, Steve Barrett, Tobie Garrick, Amy Vecchione, Troy Reeves, Carolyn Bowler, Phyllis Lyons, and Linda Morton Keithley of ISHS; Jody Hawley Ochoa and Emily Peeso of the Historical Museum; and Alan Virta and Mary Carter of BSU. Their superb contributions to Idaho and Boise history are works in progress every day. Their collection and care of photographs, images, and records are of incalculable value to Idaho citizens.

Thanks to Rick Sayre of the Hewes Library, Monmouth College, Monmouth, Illinois; to Judy Tew of Houma, Louisiana; and to Eve Chandler, Kerry Moosman, Jack Wilkerson, Marilyn Shuler, Jeanette Germain, Danna Anjevine, Pete Wilson, Kelly Mitchell, Sarah Tregay, Amy Stahl, Ron and Suzanne Joyner of Lansing, North Carolina, and Maxine Hoene. Thanks to the librarians at Boise High School. The members of the Julia Davis Park Celebration Committee reminded me in many ways why this research matters. Many others helped along the way, sometimes just by listening or pointing out research ideas. My thanks to all of you. Janet Ward, thank you for William Brabb's journal!

I'm grateful for many kinds of help from several descendants of the McCrum and Davis families. Linda Davis Leonard joined me at the Ada County Courthouse to examine deed records, an errand that grew to consume many, many hours because Tom Davis proved to be a major buyer and seller of real estate. Historians sometimes find blind alleys, but this pathway turned into a major collector.

I had a chance to meet and talk with several present-day Davis and McCrum descendants. They talked about the oral traditions and beliefs about Tom and Julia that are still alive today. Thanks to Diane Mykelgard, Linda Leonard, Marcy Haines, and Shannon Sullivan.

Leslie (McCrum) Frazho of Richmond, Virginia, has been gathering genealogical data from the many branches of the McCrum and Davis families for a long time, and she shared it. Thanks to her, we are able to correct certain previously-held beliefs, such as that Mary Thibado was Julia McCrum's "aunt."

Leslie and Holly (Davis) Taylor of Burton, Washington, Diane Davis Mykelgard, and Linda Davis Leonard all permitted the use and publication of their family photographs. Thanks to them, present and future Boiseans can visually "attach" Julia Davis to her own ancestors. Mr. and Mrs. Claycomb can at last reveal to us their kind faces.

One tries to avoid errors of fact and interpretation. Any that appear in this work are my own responsibility.

The sponsor of this book is Diane Davis Mykelgard, who probably didn't dream that she would someday require a business card as the major factor in T&J Publishing. In addition to her comprehensive vision for improvements to Julia Davis Park and a design competition to that end, the Centennial Celebration, which occurred in Julia Davis Park on June 23, 2007, and a major gathering of the Davis and McCrum families on that same date, she managed to organize and publish *The Resurrection of the Bar O: The Story of Tom and Jemima Davis* (her parents). She chaired the Centennial Celebration Committee. With all those projects and preparations underway simultaneously, she managed to supply huge quantities of optimism about this book. I thank her most humbly for the faith she placed in me.

Years ago, Jim Leonard told me that he was married to Linda Davis, a great-granddaughter of Tom and Julia Davis. He introduced me to the idea that Tom and Julia might become the subject of a book. It has, indeed, and I thank him for that first step on the path.

Book-writing is hard on spouses. The book-writer regularly neglects certain chores. Dinner is not always the well-balanced event it has been known to be. Piles of stuff accumulate in the so-called common areas of the house. Spouses deserve the last and best paragraph of thanks because they are forgiving and supportive no matter what. Thank you, Ralph.

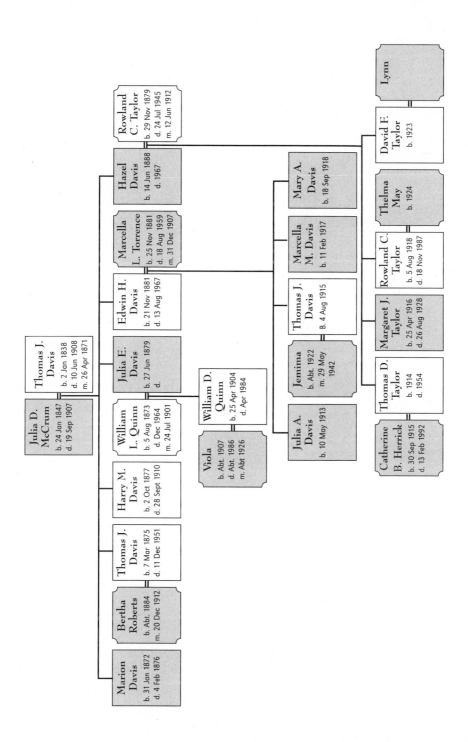

Note: This selection includes items that came to light while the author researched the biography of Tom and Julia Davis. It is neither complete nor comprehensive, but is provided as encouragement for some future historian to write a biography of the park.

1906-07   *Polk's Directory* for Boise lists the city's "parks" as: Agricultural Park (south side, Boise River), Cadet Park (¼ mile east of Boise Barracks on the Idaho City Road at Cottonwood Creek), City Driving Park (south side of Boise River, 1.5 mile west of the city), Ellis Park (20 acres near 23rd Street and Heron Avenue), Fair Grounds, Pleasure Park (south side of Warm Springs Avenue, east of Natatorium), Riverside (Miller Street between 10th and 12th streets), Harrison Boulevard.

1899   Tom and Julia offer to Boise City part of their orchard lands for a park. Boise City does not act.

1907   February 22. Tom Davis prepares deed of gift of park land to Boise City.

1907   September 19. Julia McCrum Davis dies.

1907   November 22. Boise City pays $1 for gift from Thomas Davis of "40 acres more or less" for a park to be known "always and forever" as Julia Davis Park.

1908   June 10. Thomas Davis dies.

1908-18   City fills low ground, builds concrete retaining wall, plants turf and climbing roses, builds lagoon.

1910   Circa. Mayor W.E. Pierce plants a Kentucky Coffee Bean tree in the park.

1912   Arthur L. Park creates general development plan for Julia Davis Park. It forms basis for early grading, done with horse and fresno.

1916   Zoo begins, possibly with monkey that escapes from the circus and is found in the Mountain Home desert, but more certainly when Sportsman's Club of Boise donates a collection of live game birds to the city. Birds go to Park Department, headquartered at Julia Davis.

1922-32   Davis Estate donates more land for the park on Nov 15, 1922; June 25, 1929; May 20, 1931; May 12, 1932.

1928   Bandshell is constructed.

1929   January 1. J.T. McLeod becomes superintendent of Boise Park Department. Mobilizes Works Project Administration (WPA) and other relief programs in the 1930s to plant shrubs, move drive closer to river bank, enlarge ponds, build fence.

1929   Zoo housed wolf, coyotes, brown bears, cougars, wildcats, badger, raccoons, white tailed deer, black tailed deer, elk, Rhesus monkeys, pheasants, swans, geese, wild ducks, owls, golden eagles.

1929   McLeod resurfaces six adobe-surfaced tennis courts with clay. An additional six already were in clay.

1930   Sept. 26. McLeod orders 100 Eulalia japonica gracillis at total cost of $15.

1931   February 20. Morrison-Knudsen donates old gravel pit and surrounding area for the park. Pit is added to lagoon. Boat house follows.

1931   May. Mrs. Frank D'Amant, the Idle Six, and fraternal organizations donate and dedicate 43 trees to the park. D'Amant donates 100 rose bushes from her garden.

1930-41 Circa. C.C. Anderson, owner of Golden Rule stores, sponsors annual back-to-school parade (ending at Julia Davis Park), picnic, and watermelon feed.

1931   Morrison-Knudsen Company builds Capitol Boulevard's Memorial Bridge.

1934   *Idaho Daily Statesman* moves Coston and Pierce cabins into park as basis of Pioneer Village. Columbian Club plants trees and shrubs.

1935   Members of Cut Worms, men's garden club, form idea to install a rose garden.

1937   Boise Art Association work with City of Boise and WPA to build Boise Gallery of Art.

1938   Rose Garden layout designed by McLeod, park superintendent and member of Cut Worms. WPA aids work.

1939   Rose Garden is dedicated. Contains roses from Jackson-Perkins, Villa Nurseries (Portland), and local garden clubs.

1939   July 23. Pioneer Department of the *Idaho Daily Statesman* officially presents Pioneer Village to Boise on 75th anniversary of the paper. Village is located along river near (later) Bob Gibb Friendship Bridge.

1940-41 Park is extended to Capitol Boulevard and Broadway Avenue. Lawns and shrubs planted in spring of 1941.

1941   September 30. Boise City gives State of Idaho 99-year lease for Idaho State Historical Museum. Ground is broken. World War II interrupts construction.

1941   Most meat-eating zoo animals are disposed of, due to meat rationing during World War II.

1948   August 15. Boise City Band plays Tchaikovsky's 1812 *Overture*.

1950   Idaho State Historical Museum opens.

1954   September. Arts and Crafts Festival begins, aiming to showcase local artists.

1958   Boise City Council permits "Pleasureland" concession: children's rides and entertainment. After 1966, known as "Fun Spot."

1959   November 14. Union Pacific donates engine no. 2295, "Big Mike," to Boise. It is placed in Julia Davis Park.

1960   Upon proposal to build Interstate "Connector" through Julia Davis Park, protests prevail and preserve park.

1961   Idaho Zoological Society is formed to support zoo. Planning begins.

1962   Zoo gets a caretaker with zoo experience.

1963   Boise's planning consultant, Harold E. Atkinson, suggests that the city create a "continuous green belt" of public park land along the Boise River.

1966   January 24. Greenbelt becomes official city goal.

1967   Park facilities connect to city sewer system by means of pump station.

1966-67 Hippies, "rowdies," mooning, love-ins, teenage bands show up in Julia Davis Park.

1968   October 6. Pete Seeger performs at Bandshell for crowd of 3,000 people.

1968-69 Children's Zoo opens, with financial help from Junior League.

1969   Pioneer Village is relocated east of Idaho State Historical Museum.

1969   New boathouse.

1970   The park contains over 1,000 mature trees. Park director, Gordon Bowen, reported one million visits each year, of which 25% were by people outside Ada County. Boise park system includes 36 parks.

1971   Logan house and, later, Adelman house become part of Pioneer Village.

1972   Boise Gallery of Art expands.

1973   Capitol Boulevard entrance to park is aligned with Battery Street and given a traffic signal.

1970-73 Pioneer Village moves east of Historical Museum. Logan Adobe House and iron fence from Idaho Soldier's Home are added.

1970s   Comprehensive planning exercise takes place. Roads and parking lots are rearranged.

1978   Tour Train arrives. Depot is near Pioneer Village.

1979   Memorial Rose Fund created.

1980   Bob Gibb Friendship Bridge (footbridge) over Boise River connects park to campus of Boise State University.

1981   End of lease for Fun Spot. Playground replaces it.

1982   Idaho State Historical Museum is expanded.

1986   Boise Gallery of Art is renovated and renamed Boise Art Museum.

1990   September. Bandshell rededicated.

1997   Boise Art Museum expanded to 34,800 square feet.

1998   September. Congregation of St. Paul Baptist Church moves church to the park to house Idaho Black History Museum.

1999   March 8. Dedication of Idaho Black History Museum.

2001   June. Bandshell rededicated to Gene Harris, great American jazz pianist and Boise resident.

2002   August 4. Julia Davis memorial sculpture dedicated.

2007   June 23. Celebration of the Centennial of Julia Davis Park.

SOURCES

Ada County Deed Records, Office of the Recorder, Ada County Courthouse, Boise.

City Council Minutes, Boise City Hall, Boise.

Bowen, Gordon S. *Boise Parks: A Cause and a Trust.* Boise: 2002.

Neil, J.M. *Discovering Our Surroundings.* Ms. 2/1436. Idaho State Historical Society
Public Archives and Research Library, Boise.

R.L. Polk & Co.'s Boise City & Ada County Directory, 1906-07 (and others). Salt Lake
City: R.L. Polk & Co.

www.cityofboise.org/parks

From *Idaho [Daily] Statesman*:

May 5, 1918   Mrs. E.J. Dockery, "Julia Davis Park Gives Promise of Becoming
Spot of Rare Beauty," p. 8.

July 1, 1928   Clyde Smith, "Boise's Beauty Keeps on Growing," sec. 2, p. 1.

May 12, 1940   "Park in Boise Gets Marker at Unveiling," p. 8.

June 22, 1941   Bert Eustis, "Julia Davis Park Boise Recreation Mecca," p. 12.

Sept. 11, 1960   Nellie Ireton Mills, "Apple Blossoms Laid Foundation for Julia
Davis Park Gift to City," Women's and Features section, p. 11.

Sept. 26, 1960   "Davis Descendants Pledge All-Out Fight to Save Park," p. 8.

Aug. 24, 1969   Grace Barringer, "History Grows on Trees in City's Julia Davis
Park," p. 12-C.

May 17, 1984   Arthur Hart, "Tom and Julia Davis left legacy of green," p. D-3.

Feb. 26, 1988   Renee Villeneuve, "Boise Park's Columns Found."

– *Notes* –

ABBREVIATIONS

IDS   *Idaho Tri-Weekly Statesman* (July 26, 1864 – Dec. 31, 1887), *Idaho Daily Statesman* (Jan. 1, 1888 – May 31, 1969), and *Idaho Statesman* (June 1, 1969 – present)

ISHS   Idaho State Historical Society Public Archives and Research Library, Boise, Idaho

Ms.   Manuscript

OH   Idaho Oral History Center, Boise, Idaho

PRELUDE, AN ORCHARD

1. R.Z. Johnson, ed., *Idaho, the Gem of the Mountains* (Chicago: Lewis Publishing Co., 1899), p. 121.
2. Arthur Hart, "Orchards Paid Off for Early Farmers," *IDS,* October 16, 1972, p. 12.
3. Nellie Ireton Mills, "Apple Blossoms Laid Foundation for Julia Davis Park Gift to City," *IDS,* September 11, 1960, Women's and Features section, p. 11.
4. "Davis Orchard Produces First Apples in City," undated clipping from *IDS* in Davis family scrapbook, courtesy of Diane Davis Myklegard. For description of Red June apples, see www.bighorsecreekfarm.com.

Chapter One, The Sons of Mary Ann Davis

1. The birth year of either Davis boy is difficult to say with confidence. Mrs. Claycomb gave Tom a Bible and inscribed the date of his birth as January 2, 1836. (If she gave Frank a Bible, it is yet to be found.) Later census enumerators cited Tom's birth year variously as 1836, 1839, and 1840, presumably information given by Tom himself. His obituary and gravestone settled on January 2, 1838, as did most Idaho biographers. Frank, too, has no certain birth year; it appears in census reports as 1838, 1840, and 1841. His gravestone says 1838. As there is no debate that Tom was the elder brother, it seems reasonable to proceed with the story of his life by siding with Mrs. Claycomb and assuming Tom's birth year as 1836, Frank's as 1838. Bible page courtesy of Holly Taylor; see *U.S. Census of Population* for 1850 and same for 1860 in Illinois; 1870 and 1880 in Idaho. Gravestones for Tom and Frank are in Pioneer Cemetery in Boise.

2. Military tracts were reserved for veterans of the War of 1812 as a form of payment to volunteer soldiers.

3. The cadastral survey, performed in Illinois and later in Idaho, measures land in "ranges" that stretch east and west from a meridian. One range is six miles wide. The north to south measure begins at a "base line;" each six miles is called a township.

4. Rebecca Burlend and Edward Burlend, *A True Picture of Emigration,* reprint (Lincoln: University of Nebraska Press, 1987), p. 117.

5. "John Davis Personal Estate, Bill of Appraisement," Probate records for John Davis, Warren County, Illinois. Undated, circa October 1839.

6. "John Davis Personal Estate, Bill of Appraisement."

7. "Article of Agreement" between John Davis and Polaski Skovil, July 12, 1838. Probate records, Warren County.

8. "John Davis Bill to Pulaski Scovil," August 29, 1839. Probate records, Warren County. The date indicates that John Davis had not died prior to that date.

9. "John Davis Estate Administrators' Bond," October 26, 1839, Probate records, Warren County.

10. Burlend, *A True Picture of Emigration,* p. 89-90.

11. "Bonding Court Order," November 26, 1840. Bonding records, Warren County.

12. "Coldbrook: First Settlers from Kentucky," *Salute to Area Towns,* Volume II, p. 23. See also "Do You Remember? Away Back When," September 19, no year cited, found in Moffitt Book, Volume 4, page 210, which says Claycomb arrived in Warren County in 1835.

13. Richard J. Jensen, *Illinois, A History* (Urbana: University of Illinois Press, 1978), p. 34.

14. Esquire: "Coldbrook," found at www.usgennet.org/usa/il/county/warren/cold brooktwp.html.

15. Miller marriage: Warren County Female Marriage Index; "John Miller's Estate Inventory," December 20, 1848. Probate records, Warren County, John Miller; *U.S. Census of Population,* Warren County, Illinois, 1850.

16. Information on the Claycombs, Warren County, and Monmouth are found in issues of the *Monmouth Atlas,* as extracted at www.mhrising.com/newspapers/ monmouth.

17. "Father:" Tom Davis to Julia Davis, letter, December 24, 1873, courtesy of Linda Davis Leonard and Diane Davis Mykelgard, Boise. The *U.S. Census of Population* of 1880 for Warren County lists fifteen-year-old Charles Davis, son of Hester and Frank, as part of the Claycomb household.

18. Davis family oral tradition, Diane Davis Mykelgard.

19. *U.S Census of Population,* 1860, Warren County, Illinois. Mary Ann was once more using the name Davis.

20. *Monmouth Atlas,* April 26, 1861.

CHAPTER TWO, IDAHO

1. See Merrill J. Mattes, *Platte River Road Narratives* (Urbana: University of Illinois, 1988), p.536-541; and Charles Neider, *The Complete Travel Books of Mark Twain* (Garden City, New York: Doubleday and Co., Inc., 1966), p. xi.

2. Mary Davis household, *U.S. Census of Population, 1860,* Warren County, Illinois, population schedule, Monmouth Township, page 199, dwelling 1381, family 1388.

3. See, for example, Johnson, *Idaho, Gem of the Mountains,* p. 120-121, James H. Hawley, *History of Idaho* (Chicago: S.J. Clarke Publishing Company, 1920), p. 38-44; Hiram French, *History of Idaho* (Chicago: Lewis Publishing Co., 1914), p. 709. Marcella Davis Sullivan, "An Illustrious Entrepreneur of Idaho," April 4, 1980 (unpublished manuscript), said the brothers' journey included Elk City, Walla Walla, Auburn, and Idaho City. Some sources (for example, "Prominent Boise Man Dead," *IDS,* June 11, 1908, p. 5, col. 1) say the brothers left Illinois in 1862. However, a departure date in that year would have made for an unreasonably rapid traverse from Elk City to Walla Walla to Auburn to Idaho City, where it is certain that they spent the winter of 1862-63.

4. See Johnson, p. 120; Hawley, p. 38; French, p. 709. The "bad Mormons" story also is told by Marcella Davis Sullivan in "An Illustrious Entrepreneur," April 4, 1980 (unpublished manuscript). For Fort Hall and 1861 abandonment, see Ross Cramer, *California-Oregon Trail, Fort Hall to Goose Creek, Idaho* (Burley, Idaho: U.S. Dept. of the Interior, Bureau of Land Management, 1973), p. 8-9.

5. In the 1860s, this trail was the most direct route between Darby, Montana, and Elk City, a stretch of 117 miles where no travel services are available even in 2007. The one-lane road is primitive, steep, and winding, an auto journey of ten hours. See Ernst Peterson, "Retracing the Southern Nez Perce Trail with Rev. Samuel Parker," *Montana Magazine* (Vol 16, No. 4), p. 12-27. Snowstorm: Johnson, *Idaho, Gem of the Mountains,* p. 21.

6. "Mining in Idaho," ISHS Reference Series No. 9, revised 1985. Marcella Sullivan reported that the Davis brothers intended to go to Florence. See also Mills, "Apple Blossoms."

7. "Frank R. Coffin Tells of Early Days in Famous Camp," *IDS* clipping, no date, found at ISHS Ms. 521, Papers of Frank R. Coffin, File 6, Scrapbook.

8. Elijah Lafayette Bristow. Letter to Brother, July 10, 1862, "Copies of letters, 1857-1864," ISHS Ms. 2/47. Frank Coffin was known in Boise for his many oral and written stories of the pioneers' "early days." Had the Davis brothers spent that winter in Florence, it seems likely he would have mentioned it.

9. James C. Hutton. Letter to Julia, Father, and Mother, July 29, 1862. ISHS Ms. 2/142.

10. Hawley, *History of Idaho,* p. 38.

11. Verne Bright, "Blue Mountain Eldorados: Auburn, 1861," *Oregon Historical Quarterly,* September 1961, p. 225. See also bakercounty.net/towns/auburn.htm.

12. "The Homestead Act of 1862," 37th Congress, Sess. II, 1862, approved May 20, 1862, Section 2.

13. Bristow to Tom, November 29 and 30, 1862.

14. Bristow to Willard, January 7, 1863.

15. Frank R. Coffin, "Reminiscences of Early Days in Idaho," ISHS Ms. 521, File 6.

16. "Lucky Well Digger Finds Gold in Basin," *IDS,* December 23, 1923, sec. 2, p. 2. See also Johnson, *Idaho, Gem of the Mountains,* p. 61.

17. "Lucky Well Digger;" Merle W. Wells, *Gold Camps and Silver Cities* (Moscow, Idaho: Idaho Department of Lands, Bureau of Mines and Geology, Bulletin 22, 2nd edition, 1983), p. 4-5.

18. Partners: Hester Cory Davis, "Pioneers Enjoy Fresh Milk and Butter En Route," *IDS,* June 8, 1930, sec. 2, p. 2, col. 1-2. The Claim $5,000: Sullivan, "Illustrious Entrepreneur"; arrivals: Wells, *Gold Camps,* p. 4-5.

19. Wells, *Gold Camps,* p. 6-7.

20. Annie Laurie Bird, *Boise, the Peace Valley* (Caldwell: Caxton Printers, 1934), p. 188-89. "Cap" was likely Donald McKay, son of Thomas McKay. Thomas McKay was the Hudson Bay trapper.

21. Eugene B. Chaffee, *Early History of the Boise Region, 1811-1864* (University of California Masters Thesis, circa 1952), p. 62.

CHAPTER THREE, BOISE

1. Bird, quoting Sherlock Bristol in *Boise, The Peace Valley,* p. 181; Littel: Louis A. Boas, "Man in whose Cabin Boise Was Born, Dies Near Moscow," *IDS,* June 6, 1962, sec. 2, p. 2, col. 1.

2. Chaffee, *Early History of Boise Region,* p. 55-56; Ritchey, as quoted in Bird, Boise, The Peace Valley, p. 188.

3. Bird, quoting Hester Corey Davis in *Boise, The Peace Valley,* p. 188-189. See also Chaffee, *Early History of Boise Region,* p. 62-63.

4. Bird, quoting William Ritchey in *Boise, The Peace Valley,* p. 188. Part of the account was printed as "Man in Whose Cabin Boise Was Born, Dies Near Moscow."

5. Farmers' Co-operative Ditch Co. vs. Riverside Irrigation District, Ltd. *Transcript on Appeal from the District Court to the Seventh Judicial District of the State of Idaho, in and for the County of Canyon, 1909,* volumes I and II, p. 1526. Hereafter cited as *Transcript.*

6. Thomas Davis testimony, *Transcript,* p. 1079.

7. Bird, *Boise, The Peace Valley,* p. 200-201.

8. "Lucky Well Digger."

9. Mills, "Apple Blossoms."

10. "Just Why was Fort Boise Established?", *IDS,* April 8, 1923, Sec. 2, p. 2, col. 1.

11. Chaffee, *Early History of Boise Region,* p. 64-69.

12. Chaffee, *Early History of Boise Region,* p. 69-70. Lugenbeel reserved 638 acres for the post, 503 for the hay reserve, 343 for wood, and 632 for the sawmill. The name of the fort was changed to Boise Barracks on April 5, 1879.

13. Bird, *Boise, The Peace Valley,* p. 189. The distinction between the "incorporators" and the "members" of the townsite company is hard to discern. The plat identifies twenty individuals among whom the 120 lots were distributed. Sources differ as to the "incorporators." Chaffee, quoting Ritchey, listed Sherlock Bristol, Frank Davis, Ike Dymes, H.C. Riggs, J.D. Agnew, "Cap" Hines, M.N. Beel, and W.L. Ritchey. Hawley listed them as H.C. Riggs, James D. Agnew, B.M. DuRell, George D. Ellis, Barrett Williams, John Lemp, Matthew H. Williams, Frank Davis, and Tom Davis.

14. Lugenbeel quote: Bird, *Boise, The Peace Valley,* p. 195. Mrs. Cyrus Jacobs gave the original plat to ISHS in 1907.

15. See Ada County Tax Collection records at ISHS.

16. Hawley, *History of Idaho,* p. 688.

17. "Henry Chile Riggs," ISHS Reference Series No. 595, 1981. See also, Hawley, *History of Idaho,* p. 691.

18. "Eden:" W.M. Brabb, *Diary kept by W.M. Brabb while traveling from Shelbina, Missouri, to Pendleton, Oregon, 1882.* Copy at Special Collections, Albertsons

Library, Boise State University, Boise, Idaho. McClellan's ferry is believed to have crossed the river near modern-day Ninth Street Bridge.

19. Chaffee, *Early History of Boise Region*, p. 71. See also, "Boise, City of Trees, A Centennial History," ISHS Reference Series no. 12 (Boise, ISHS, 1963), p. 5. Charles May came with Lugenbeel to erect brick structures at the Fort. In 1866, May built a sandstone structure for Cyrus Jacobs.

20. Sandstone houses and labor: Chaffee, *Early History of Boise Region*, p. 72-73, and *IDS*, Sept 9, 1945, p. 7, col 1. Population: "Boise City and Urban Area Population, 1863-1980," ISHS Reference Series No. 363, revised 1995.

21. Nine hours: "Idaho and Boise City Stage Line. Ward and Co. (advertisement)," *Idaho Directory*, November 26, 1864; toll road: Larry Jones, "Boise-Idaho City Toll Road," ISHS Reference Series No. 78, 1977.

22. Jones, "Toll Road," p. 3. "Fifteen Miles" probably refers to its distance from Idaho City.

Chapter Four, Apples

1. "George D. Ellis is Called by Death," *IDS*, April 13, 1911, p. 5. The acreage around Ellis's home eventually annexed to Boise City as the Ellis Addition; Ada County Deed Book No. 1, p. 390, August 24, 1867, Ada County Recorder, Boise, Idaho. Ritchey sold his interest "in a certain ranch or farm commonly known as Davis and Ritchey Ranch" to Tom Davis, Frank Davis, and George Ellis for $6,000.

2. Arthur Hart, "Water Wheels Gave Boise Valley a Lift," *IDS*, February 26, 1973, p. 11, col. 1.

3. Hawley, *History of Idaho*, p. 370.

4. Chaffee, *Early History of Boise Region*, p. 76. See also "Henry Chiles Riggs," ISHS Reference Series No. 595,

5. Chaffee, *Early History of Boise Region*, p. 78, quoting Idaho City's Idaho World of December 17, 1864.

6. Chaffee, *Early History of Boise Region*, p. 75-90, recounts the story of the shift of the capitol from Lewiston to Boise.

7. "Report from Idaho City," *IDS*, August 20, 1864, p. 3, col. 1.

8. Ada County Deed Book No. 1, pages 29, 275, 246, 597, and 326, respectively.

9. Ada County Deed Book No. 2, p. 201. Stilts bought 25 feet of frontage on Lot 3 in Block 4 on February 20, 1867. Prior to that he may have leased. The image is at ISHS Library, No. 73.

10. Taxes, trees: "Boise, City of Trees," p. 5; improvements, hospital, cats: Johnson, *Idaho, Gem of the Mountains*, p. 62-64, 336; toll road: *IDS*, November 12, 1864.

11. "Boise City Charter," ISHS Reference Series No. 30; Sue Paseman and Todd Shallat, "Boise's Two-Month Mayor: Henry Prickett," at www.boisestate.edu, "Mayoral Albums; Hawley, *History of Idaho*, p. 688.

12. Ada County Deed Book No. 3, p. 674, 676.

13. By government survey, the ranch between the city plat and the river amounted to 153.7 acres, located in Section 10 of T3N, R2E, fractions 3, 4, 5, and 10. See Preemption Certificate No. 2, Serial No. 29964, October 5, 1869, signed by President Ulysses S. Grant.

14. French, *History of Idaho*, p. 709.

15. Liping Zhu, *A Chinaman's Chance* (Boulder: University of Colorado Press, 1997), p. 55.

16. *U.S. Census of Population*, 1870 for Boise City, Schedule 3, Productions of Agriculture, page 18.

17. The men were Richard Jewell, 63, "works on farm;" Phillip Pencil, 25, stage driver; Owen Langford, 40, "without occupation." See *U.S. Census of Population, Idaho*, 1870, page 63.

Chapter Five, Women

1. Reynolds: "Emigrants," *IDS*, August 16, 1894, p. 2, col. 1.

2. Hester Davis' story is in "Pioneers Enjoy Fresh Milk and Butter En Route," *IDS*, June 8, 1930, Sec. 2, p. 2.

3. Crickets: Mrs. James Davis Agnew, "Idaho Pioneers of 1864," *Washington Historical Quarterly* 15 (No. 1, January 1924), p. 44.

4. "Emigrants," *IDS*, August 16, 1864, p. 2, col. 1; "A Word to Immigrants," *IDS*, August 20, 1864, p. 2, col. 2.

5. "Dancing Party on Tuesday Night," *IDS*, November 10, 1864, p. 2, col. 3; population: ISHS Reference Series No. 363.

6. Wedding: "Married," *Idaho World*, January 21, 1865, p. 2, col. 5.

7. Bird, *Boise, The Peace Valley*, p. 188. Frank and Hester sold the house to William N. Nye on April 3, 1877 for $3,000 in gold coin. The property fronted both Front and Grove streets: lots 4, 5, 10, and parts of lots 11, 3, and 9 in Block 22. See Ada County Deed Book No. 7, p. 324. The *U.S. Census of Population* for Ada County for 1870, p. 51, recorded the other three in the house as Sarah C. Johnson, 26, a "music teacher;" Sarah and Alice Simpson, 16 and 12. Pickel was 28. Sarah Johnson probably was one of the children raised by Harriet Ann and Andrew Claycomb. See "Do you remember? Away back when," Moffitt Book, vol. 4, p. 210, which recalled the obituary of Andrew Claycomb.

8. "The Party at the Overland," *IDS*, February 19, 1874, p. 3, col. 1.

9. Frank's purchase: Ada County Deed Book No. 6, p. 172. Samuel Orr, who had not completed patent procedures, sold the land to Frank Davis on January 18, 1870. Frank eventually acquired a patent on May 5, 1875, under the First Morrill Act, for $1.25 per acre. Today, the land is bounded by 20th, 28th, Anderson, and Heron streets; "Locust Grove Dairy Farm," advertisement in *IDS*, April 30, 1885, p. 2, col. 3.

10. "Another Veteran Goes," *IDS*, April 29, 1871, p. 3, col 1.

11. Chess: Arthur Hart, "Tom and Julia Davis left legacy of green," *IDS*, May 17, 1984, p. D-3; Knox: Thomas Donaldson, *Idaho of Yesterday* (Caldwell: Caxton Printers, 1941), p. 69, under subheading, "Northwest Liars and their Lies."

12. See cambridgeweb.net/historical/galt.html. Galt is now part of the city of Cambridge near Kitchener. It is roughly north of Erie, Pennsylvania, across Lake Erie.

13. Absolom Shade: entry at www.wikipedia.com; Henry McCrum: Family Group Sheet, Henry McCrum (I), courtesy of Leslie Frazho. See also cambridgeweb. net/historical/galt.html.

14. Batters: Family Group Sheet, "William Batters," and personal communication, July 25, 2007, courtesy of Leslie Frazho. William Batters died in Ontario in 1853. See also Rosalie Stringfellow, "Boise's Beautiful Park is Memorial to Pioneer Julia Davis," *IDS*, August 22, 1943, p. 8, col. 3, and Mills, "Apple Blossoms."

15. Julia's parents: Henry McCrum II and Marion N. Batters were named after a father or mother respectively. Source: Family Group Sheet "Marion Neilson Batters" courtesy of Leslie Frazho. Names such as Henry, Marion, Julia, Etta, Richard, and others continue to pass down the McCrum family. The obituary for Julia's mother said that the McCrum family home was at the head of Spruce Street and adjoining the Stone Road.

16. "Henry McCrum III," Family Group Sheet, courtesy of Leslie Frazho.

17. Stringfellow, "Boise's Beautiful Park." Sources variously spell the name Thibado as Thibodo, Thibido, and Thibideau.

18. Coroner: "Ada County Officials, 1865 to 1885," found at www.gesswhoto.com/idaho/ada-county-officials.html.

19. Predicament: Dick Barrett, "Descendants of Thomas Jefferson Davis, Generation No. 1," p. 1, unpublished manuscript provided by Leslie Frazho; wedding: Western States Marriage Record Index. Vol. 1, p. 72.ID No. 1179.

20. "Fine Orchard," *IDS*, May 19, 1870, p. 3, col. 1. Also referenced in George Yost and Dick d'Easum, *Idaho: The Fruitful Land* (Boise: Syms-York Company, 1980), p. 23.

21. Mills, "Apple Blossoms."

22. Pickel: *IDS*, April 29, 1871, p. 3, col. 3. Hester Davis' obituary said Hester was at the center of social life in the 1860s, that despite her mere one hundred pounds,

she had the strength and determination to do the work of a man. She was "heroic," a "good businesswoman," a "lovable character, kind and generous," had "unusual mental gifts, a clean and active mind," and used her "well-earned substance" to make others comfortable. See *IDS*, Sept 26, 1937. She was widowed in 1891, when Frank died of cancer. She carried on the business of the dairy and eventually subdivided it as Boise grew westward, creating the Pleasanton, Frank Davis, and Hester Davis additions.

Chapter Six, Marion

1. Weather: No title ("Mr. Carrey says..."), *IDS*, February 5, 1874, p. 3, col. 1.
2. While researching this book, the author learned that Kerry Moosman, an Idaho resident, possessed a letter written by Tom Davis. Mr. Moosman generously provided the letter to the Davis family. This transcription provides punctuation and paragraph breaks for readers' convenience.
3. No title, *IDS*, February 28, 1874, p. 3, col. 1.
4. Ada County Deed Book No. 6, p. 333, December 12, 1874. He bought the 160 acres (in T4N R2E, parts of secs 27 and 34) from Asa McCully for $4,500.
5. Thomas C. Elgas, *Nevada, Official Centennial Book* (Las Vegas: Nevada Publications, 1976), p. 426.
6. "Roseola," *IDS*, February 1, 1876, p. 3, col. 1.
7. "Sad," *IDS*, February 5, 1876, p. 3, col 1.
8. "Died," *IDS*, February 8, 1876, p. 3, col. 3.

Chapter Seven, Cattle

1. Charles McCrum: "Pioneer called to final reward," *IDS*, September 14, 1919, p. 5, col. 3; sasparilla: personal communication to author from Leslie Frazho; parties: see for example, "Weeks News Socially," *IDS*, January 28, 1895, p. 4, col. 4. The two were among fifty women at an afternoon reception at the home of Mrs. Whitehead.
2. *U.S. Census of Population*, Ada County, 1880.
3. "Gone East," *IDS*, May 7, 1881, p. 3, col. 1. Mrs. McCrum traveled east on the Overland Stage.
4. Julia's generosity: Hawley, *History of Idaho*, Vol. 2, p. 43; Oregon Trail travelers: Mrs. Agnew said that her own party had little money, that their stock had died en route, and that many who stayed in Boise lived in dugouts in the foothills. See Agnew, "Idaho Pioneers of 1864," p. 47.
5. Brabb, *Diary*, p. 72.
6. Brabb, *Diary*, p. 73-74.

7. Zhu, quoting an *IDS* article of September 14, 1865, in *Chinaman's Chance,* note 59, p. 30-31.

8. Zhu, *Chinaman's Chance,* p. 111.

9. Zhu, *Chinaman's Chance,* p. 113-114.

10. Stringfellow, "Boise's Beautiful Park," writing in 1943, believed that Tom Davis "brought the first Chinese gardeners to Boise and treated them well."

11. "Married. McCrum-Cartee," *IDS* December 17, 1881, p. 5, col. 1.

12. "Local," *IDS,* October 11, 1877, p. 3, col. 1; "Pickles and Green Corn," *IDS,* October 30, 1877, p. 3, col. 1. The editor wrote that Tom had "large experience in putting up canned goods," and that these were taking the place of foreign importations; ranching: see "Local," *IDS,* October 6, 1877, p. 3, col. 1. See also Hawley, *History of Idaho,* Vol 2, p. 43. Their store was in the building later occupied by "the Delano-Thompson Shoe Company." Himrod's obituary says he worked as a bookkeeper/clerk for Cyrus Jacobs' store and Louthan & Bilderback's store between 1864 and 1878, from which we may infer the store partnership with Davis began around 1878. See "Charles Himrod, Pioneer Citizen, is called beyond," *IDS,* January 27, 1920, p. 5, col. 1.

13. Bar O: Vila Gilman Minger, "Cowboy Swims for Life As Cattle Swamp Ferry." From clipping file in Davis family scrapbook, publication and date not identified, but circa the 1930s. The two irons of an early Bar O brand are on display at the Idaho State Historical Museum. Bruneau: "A Good Winter Range," *IDS,* January 7, 1890, p. 3, col. 1-2. The Charles Himrod store journals, daily account books, letterpress book, and invoice book constitute ISHS Ms. 513. They date between 1885 and 1891.

14. Charles Himrod, ISHS Ms. 513, see for example, "Journal" for May 1885, p. 1854, a food order for Davis and McCrum; p. 1869 for a Davis household order for hats, a corset, and food items.

15. Larry Jones, "Dorsey's Ferry, Grandview Ferry," ISHS Reference Series No. 753. Dorsey owned the ferry between 1883-1887. It was replaced by a bridge in 1921. Davis and McCrum placed a large order, for example, on January 23, 1886. See Himrod, ISHS Ms. 513, "Day-Book," p. 2090.

16. Himrod, ISHS Ms. 513, "Journal, May 1885-April 1886," entry under June 18, 1885.

17. No title, *IDS,* September 23, 1886, p. 3, col. 3.

18. "Local Brevities," *IDS,* September 25, 1886, p. 3, col. 1.

19. "Ranching and Mining in the Bruneau Country," ISHS Reference Series No. 503, 1973, p. 1.

20. Henry Ott testimony, *Transcript,* p. 1075. See also "Just Why was Fort Boise Established?", *IDS,* April 8, 1923.

21. Land assembly: Henry Ott, *Transcript,* p. 1075-1076. See also Ada County Deed Book No. 16, page 546, October 16, 1890. John and Martha Gakey sold 93 acres to Thomas Davis for $7,000. Chinese: Thomas J. Davis, May 18, 1978, oral history by interviewer, A.W. Dawson, ISHS OH 496, p. 10.

22. Homesteading: Gratia Bacon Matthews, *Round Valley, My Home in Covered Wagon Days* (USA: Matthews, 1981), p. 22; Arthur Hart, "Payette Lake area's beauty, wildlife enchanted visitors," *IDS,* April 3, 1989, p. 3-D. John Nasi, interviewed by Joe Bennett in ISHS OH No. 431, May 13, 1971, believed Davis acquired Long Valley property in 1898 date, but Thomas J. Davis, grandson of Tom Davis, believed the ranches were acquired after 1900. See "Thomas Jefferson Davis," ISHS OH No. 496, May 18, 1978.

23. James Macdonald and James Sinclair, *History of Hereford Cattle* (London: Vinton and Co., 1886), p. 310-316.

24. Hereford history found at www.ansi.okstate.edu/breeds/cattle/hereford. See also www.herefordwebpages.co.uk/herdhist.shtml.

25. Quotation: Albert (and Grace) Campbell, interviewed by Joe Bennett and Doug Jones, ISHS OH No. 410, April 1, 1976.

Chapter Eight, Leading Citizen

1. "County Union Convention," *IDS,* August 23, 1864, p. 3, col 1.

2. "Improvement of the Public Square," *IDS,* June 2, 1877, p. 3, col. 2. Ostner made a drawing depicting the statue's dedication day, which illustrates the appearance of the square in 1869. See ISHS No. 138. In 1886, the Idaho Territorial Capitol was erected in the square.

3. "The School Tax and Public School," *IDS,* June 7, 1877, p. 2, col. 2; "The Public School," *IDS,* June 9, 1877, p. 2, col. 1.

4. "Boise City and Urban Area Population, 1863-1980," ISHS Reference Series No. 363, 1995.

5. Contemporary histories treating Boise efforts to attract a "main line" railroad include Merle Wells, *Boise: An Illustrated History* (Woodland Hills, California: Windsor Publications, 1982), Chapter 3, "In Search of a Railroad, 1868-1889;" and Carol Lynn MacGregor, *Boise, Idaho, 1882-1910, Prosperity in Isolation* (Missoula: Mountain Press Publishing Co., 2006), "The Railroad," p. 39-46. See also Thornton Waite, "Boise: On The Main Line At Last," *The Streamliner,* Union Pacific Historical Society. Found at ISHS vertical file, "Boise, Idaho — Railroad Service and Stations."

6. MacGregor, *Boise, Idaho,* p. 41.

7. "The Railroad Meeting," *IDS,* January 24, 1884, p. 3, col. 1.

8. Cartee: Ada County Deed Book No. 4, p. 383, December 2, 1870, and Book 4, p. 384-85, August 4, 1871; Flanagan: Ada County Deed Book No. 8, p. 115, January 10, 1879, and Book No. 9, p. 52, March 4, 1881.

9. Ada County Deed Book No. 10, p. 354, March 18, 1884.

10. "The Railroad Collapse," *IDS*, April 16, 1885, p. 2, col. 1.

11. "Idaho Fruit," *IDS*, September 26, 1889, p. 3, col. 1.

12. "Electric Light Company," *IDS*, October 5, 1886, p. 3, col. 1. Davis was also on the board of Artesian Water and Land Company after a water discovery in Hulls Gulch in 1890.

13. Dates: "Once the Pride of Boise," *IDS* photo caption, October 24, 1947, p. 15, col. 2. Branch: "Boise, Union Pacific Started in Same Year; Rail History Unfolded," *IDS*, July 23, 1939, p. 6, col. 1; Wells, *Boise,* p. 50-51; "Stub," MacGregor, *Boise, Idaho,* p. 42. The bench depot site was between today's Federal Way and Vista Avenue. For 1893 activity, see "The Boise Central," *IDS*, March 8, 1893, p. 8, col. 1; "A New Company," *IDS*, March 21, 1893, p. 8, col. 1; "Local Brevities," *IDS*, March 16, 1893, p. 5, col. 2; and Waite, "Boise: On the Main Line," p. 11. Passengers used the freight depot until the passenger depot opened in 1895.

14. Iron front: "Local," *IDS*, October 3, 1889, p. 3, col. 4. Davis had already fitted his own store building with an iron front in 1886, at which time he also added another storey to the building. See "Local Brevities," *IDS*, October 7, 1886, p. 3, col. 3. Orchard tour: Arthur Hart, "Boise Cleaned House in 1889," *IDS,* May 16, 1988, p. 3-D.

15. "Chips," *IDS*, September 8, 1889, p. 3, col. 1; and September 28, 1889, p. 3, col.3. The new 7th Street house was on the property occupied in 2007 by the Hampton Inn hotel at Capitol Boulevard and Myrtle Street. See also Paul Jones, "Remembering Boise, Idaho, in the Early Years of the 19th [sic] Century," who said the larger mansion stood uncompleted for twenty years before being torn down.

16. "More room; more houses," *IDS*, September 28, 1889, p. 3, col. 3. See *Boise City Directory, 1891* (Boise: Leadbetter and Walterbeck, 1891). p. 48, for McPherson's advertisement.

17. Apple shipments: "Local," *IDS*, July 26, 1890, p. 4, col. 1; prunes: "Prune Culture," October 4, 1889, p. 3, col. 1. The 1903 and 1912 *Sanborn Fire Insurance Maps* for Boise City (New York: Sanborn Map and Publishing Co., ISHS microfilm no. 0058) show the location of the new house, a small house northwest of the main house, hay storage, buggy house, fruit dryer, other (vacant) orchard-related structures, and "iron storage" (1912) buildings.

18. Plat of Davis' Addition, Ada County Recorder, Boise, Idaho, recorded May 12, 1890.

19. Plat of Central Subdivision, Ada County Recorder, Boise, Idaho, June 3, 1890.
20. Bennett: Ada County Deed Book No. 16, p. 106, July 31, 1890; Gakey: Ada County Deed Book No. 16, p, 546, October 16, 1890.
21. See map, "Boise City, Ada County, Showing Extended Limits," February 1885.
22. The Davis orchard on Crane Creek was in production at the time of Tom's death in 1908.
23. "More room, more houses."
24. Obituary: "Local Intelligence," *IDS*, March 10, 1891, p. 7, col. 2, and Ada County Probate Records, Frank M. Davis, p. 356. For Hester's plats, see Ada County Recorder. In her later years, Hester moved to Los Angeles to live with her daughter and died in September 1937 at age 95, an honored pioneer of Boise. She is buried next to her husband and her son, Charles A., who died October 30, 1903.
25. New houses: Leadbetter and Walterbeck, *Boise City Directory*, p. 15; improvements: Western Publishing Co., *Boise City, Nampa and Caldwell Directory* (Boise: 1893), p. 24.

Chapter Nine, Julia Goes to the Fair

1. Indulgent: "Prominent Boise Man Dead," *IDS*, June 11, 1908. Julia's efforts to discipline are part of the Davis family oral tradition, Diane Davis Myklegard.
2. Anthony James Miranda, *Youth and Beauty Bright, Coming of Age at Old Boise High, 1901-1921* (Boise: Miranda, 2003), p. 19.
3. See Boise High School *Courier*, Vol. VI, No. 7 (May 1906) which lists graduates from the years 1893 through 1905. Thomas is mentioned, but no other Davis siblings. The Idaho Territorial Legislature created the Independent School District of Boise on February 4, 1881. In 1889, the school offered a full four-year course for the first time. Hazel attended Fairmont School for Girls in Washington, D.C.
4. Oberlin: "Local Brevities," *IDS*, December 28, 1893, p. 6, col. 4; Harry at cow camp: Julia Davis to Edwin Davis, undated letter, addressed to Notre Dame; Harry's bad heart: "Died," *IDS*, September 29, 1910, p. 5, col. 3; drinking: Albert Campbell, April 1, 1976, ISHS OH No. 410, interviewed by Joe Bennett and Doug Jones. Harry's death notice ("Died") said he attended school in California.
5. Sullivan, "An Illustrious Entrepreneur of Idaho," p. 8.
6. Victoria Louise Eoff, "Historical Information," May 2, 1928, ISHS Ms. 356, "Columbian Club," Box 10, File 13.
7. "The Idaho Building," *IDS*, March 14, 1893, p. 8, col. 1.
8. Natatorium dance: "Local Brevities," *IDS*, March 19, 1893, p. 5. The ball was April 5, 1893. Streetcars: "Local Brevities," *IDS*, April 2, 1893, p. 8, col. 4; Davis table: "In Society's Realm," *IDS*, April 8, 1893, p. 5, col. 1.

9. City Hall: "Local Brevities," *IDS*, March 17, 1893, p. 5, col. 1, and "The New City Hall," April 29, 1863, p. 5, col. 1; railroad: "The Boise Central," *IDS*, March 8, 1893, p. 8, col. 1; "Local Brevities," *IDS*, March 16, 1893, p. 5, col. 2; "A New Company," March 21, 1893, p. 8, col. 1.

10. Horse ad: example in *IDS*, April 16, 1893, p. 2, col. 4; fruit: see, for example, "Idaho's Horticultural Exhibit," *IDS*, April 26, 1893, p. 8, col. 2.

11. Steward at-home: *IDS*, April 17, 1893, p. 8, col. 1; "The Himrod-Reed Reception," *IDS*, April 30, 1893, p. 1, col. 3.

12. Eoff, "Historical Information."

13. Insurance: "Are You Going to the World's Fair?" *IDS*, May 13, 1893, p. 4, col. 4; thru service: "World's Fair Travelers Will Have It," *IDS*, March 21, 1893, p. 2, col. 2; Wells: "Worlds Fair Notes," *IDS*, March 8, 1893, p. 8, col. 4; opals: "Idaho at the Fair," *IDS*, April 18, 1893, p. 5, col. 1.

14. Opening: "Idaho's Fruit Exhibit," *IDS*, May 2, 1893, p. 1, col. 3; "How to See Chicago," *IDS*, May 4, 1893, p. 3, col. 3; "Local Brevities," *IDS*, May 6, 1893, p. 8. On safety, see *IDS*, May 7, 1893, p. 6, col. 1.

15. "For the Free Kindergarten" and "A Dull Social Week," *IDS*, May 7, 1893, p. 5, col. 1; Relief Society: no title, *IDS*, May 10, 1893, p. 4, col. 1; "Boise Relief Society," *IDS*, May 10, 1893, p. 8, col. 1.

16. "Graduating Exercises," *IDS*, May 26, 1893, p. 1, col. 3.

17. "The Declamatory Contest," *IDS*, June 2, 1893, p. 8, col. 4.

18. "Graduating Exercises," *IDS*, June 3, 1893, p. 8, col. 1.

19. "In the Social World," *IDS*, June 5, 1893, p. 8, col. 1.

20. "Capital City Society," *IDS*, June 11, 1893, p. 5, col. 1; no title, *IDS*, July 21, 1893, p. 8, col. 4. Julia and her son left Boise on June 5.

21. Tom Davis, Sr.: "Idaho at the World's Fair," *IDS*, June 27, 1893, p. 1, col. 4; his return: "Local Brevities," *IDS*, July 21, 1893, p. 8, col. 4. Davis signed the Idaho register around June 25 and returned to Boise prior to July 21. Economy: Larson, *The Devil in the White City*, p. 240. Rails: Waite, "Boise: On the Main Line," p. 11.

22. "Idaho Visitors at the Fair," *IDS*, June 11, 1893, p. 1, col. 2. Julia and Tom, Jr., signed the Idaho register on June 10. Fair: Larson, *The Devil in the White City*, p. 250.

23. Shoup: *IDS*, June 11, 1893; "Ladies Reception Room," *IDS*, June 6, 1893, p. 5, col. 1.

24. Kathleen R. Hodges, ed., *A Light in the Window of Idaho, Boise's Public Library, 1895-1995* (Boise: Friends of the Boise Public Library, 1995), particularly Chapter Two, "Women of the Columbian Club: 1892-1905," by Suzanne Sermon, p. 17-22.

25. Impact of fair: Larson, *The Devil in the White City*, p. 274-275; new objective: Mrs. S.H. Hays, "Columbian Club," ISHS Ms. 356, Box 4, file "Committee Reports, 1898-1900."

CHAPTER TEN, THE PARK

1. Hodges, *A Light in the Window of Idaho,* p. 33-37.

2. Eulalie Northrup, "Report of the Town and Village Improvement Department," Papers of the Columbian Club, ISHS Ms. 356, Box 4, File "Committee Reports, 1892-1906."

3. See J.M. Neil, "Discovering Our Surroundings," ISHS Ms. No. 2/1436, p. 6-9.

4. Gertrude Hays, "History of the Columbian Club, 1898-1900," in IHSH Ms. 356, Box 10, File 13.

5. Minutes of the Boise City Council, September 7, 1899, Boise City Hall, Boise, Idaho.

6. Arthur Hart, "Tom and Julia Davis left legacy of green," *IDS,* May 17, 1984, p. 3-D.

7. Julia Davis. Letter to Edd, probably May 1900. Courtesy of the Davis family.

8. Etta Davis. Letter to Edd Davis, March 30, 1900. Courtesy of the Davis Family.

9. Polk, Boise City Directory 1904, p. 121; *Boise City Directory 1905,* p. 113, 163. See also Ada County Probate Records, Thomas Davis, Ada County. By that time, his shares in the Vitrified Brick operation had lost their value.

10. Geo. W. Anderson. Letter to Edwin Davis, June 15, 1900. Courtesy of the Davis family.

11. Anderson to Edwin Davis, June 15, 1900.

12. "Beautiful Wedding Ceremony," *IDS,* July 26, 1901, p. 5, col. 1.

13. Thomas J. Davis (grandson of Thomas Davis). Interviewed by A.W. Dawson, May 18, 1978, ISHS OH No. 496, p. 2,

14. "Pioneer Resident Goes Beyond," *IDS,* September 20, 1907, p. 4, col 7; "Body of Pioneer Laid to Rest," *IDS,* September 25, 1907, p. 5, col. 3.

15. Ada County Deed Book No. 74, page 62, Instrument No. 17480, November 22, 1907. See also "Thomas Davis Gives Capital City Land Along Boise River for Park," *IDS,* November 23, 1907.

16. Mrs. S.H. Hays and Mrs. L.P. McCalla, ISHS Ms. 356, Box 4, file Committee Reports.

17. Stringfellow "Boise's Beautiful Park."

18. L.P. McCalla, ISHS Ms. 356, Box 4, file Committee Reports.

19. The Davis' housekeeper and cook most likely was an African-American widow named Rebecca Davis (no relation). After Tom's death, she worked at times for Marcella Torrance Davis and Governor James Brady, among other clients, and died in 1913 at the age of 41. Marcella paid for her funeral at Morris Hill Cemetery.

20. "Body of Pioneer is at Rest," *IDS,* June 15, 1908, p. 5, col. 3.

Selected Bibliography

Books and Articles

Adams. *Idaho City: Queen of the Gold Camps*. Idaho City: Idaho World Publishing Co., 1958.

Agnew, Mrs. James Davis. "Idaho Pioneers of 1864," *Washington Historical Quarterly*, Vol. 15, No. 1 (January 1924), p. 44-48.

Ashbaugh, Don. *Nevada's Turbulent Yesterday...a Study in Ghost Towns*. Las Vegas: Westernlore Press, 1963.

Bancroft, Hubert Howe. *History of Washington, Idaho, and Montana*. San Francisco: The History Company, 1890.

Bird, Annie Laurie. *Boise the Peace Valley*. Caldwell: The Caxton Printers, 1934; reprinted in 1975.

"Boise, City of Trees: A Centennial History." Idaho State Historical Society Reference Series No. 12. Boise: 1963.

Brabb, W.M. *Diary kept by W.M. Brabb while traveling from Shelbina, Missouri, to Pendleton, Oregon, 1882*. Copy at Special Collections, Albertsons Library, Boise State University, Boise, Idaho.

Bright, Verne. "Blue Mountain Eldorados: Auburn, 1861." *Oregon Historical Quarterly* (September 1961): 213-236.

Burlend, Rebecca. *A True Picture of Emigration*. Lincoln, Nebraska: University of Nebraska Press, 1987 (reprint).

Chaffee, Eugene B. *Early History of the Boise Region, 1811-1864*. Masters Thesis, University of California, no date.

Donaldson, Thomas. *Idaho of Yesterday.* Caldwell: Caxton Printers, Ltd., 1934.

Elgas, Thomas C. *Nevada, Official Centennial Book.* Las Vegas: Nevada Publications, 1976.

Elliot, Russell R. *History of Nevada.* Lincoln: University of Nebraska Press, 1973.

Ewart, Shirley, and Jane and John Anderson. *A Long and Wearisome Journey: The Eakin Family Diaries, 1866.*

Farmers' Co-operative Ditch Co. vs. Riverside Irrigation District, Ltd. *Transcript on Appeal from the District Court to the Seventh Judicial District of the State of Idaho, in and for the County of Canyon, 1909*, volumes I and II. (Found at Idaho State Historical Library, KF1584.A2 1909.)

French, Hiram T. *History of Idaho.* Chicago: Lewis Publishing Company, 1914.

Hart, Arthur. *The Boiseans at Home.* Boise: Historic Boise, Inc., 1992, third printing.

Hartman, Hugh H. *The Founding Fathers of Boise.* Boise: Hugh Hartman, 1989.

Hawley, James H. *History of Idaho: The Gem of the Mountains, Volume II.* Chicago: S.J. Clarke Publishing Company, 1920.

Hodges, Kathleen R., ed. *A Light in the Window of Idaho, Boise's Public Library, 1895-1995.* Boise: Friends of the Boise Public Library, 1995.

"Idaho: A Brief History." ISHS Reference Series No. 7. Boise: 1962.

Jensen, Richard J. *Illinois, A History.* Urbana: University of Illinois Press, 1978.

Johnson, R.Z., ed. *Idaho, the Gem of the Mountains.* Chicago: Lewis Publishing Co., 1899.

Jones, Larry. *Boise-Idaho City Toll Road.* Boise: Idaho State Historical Society Reference Series No. 78, 1977.

Jones, Paul. *Remembering Boise, Idaho, in the Early Years of the 19th [sic] Century.* Manuscript. Courtesy Robert P. Jones, Boise, Idaho.

Larson, Erik. *The Devil in the White City.* New York: Vintage Books, Random House, 2003.

MacGregor, Carol Lynn. *Boise, Idaho, 1882-1910: Prosperity in Isolation.* Missoula, Montana: Mountain Press Publishing Company, 2006.

McDonald, James, and James Sinclair. *History of Hereford Cattle.* London: Vinton and Company, 1886. [reprint found at Cornell.edu]

Mattes, Merrill J. *Platte River Narratives, An Index to Overland Trail and California Trail Pioneers.* Urbana: University of Illinois Press, 1988.

Matthews, Gratia Bacon. *Round Valley, My Home in Covered Wagon Days.* USA: Matthews, 1981.

Mikesell, Stephen Dean. *The Golden Order, People and Government in Southwest Idaho, 1863-1867.* Honors thesis: Harvard College, 1971.

Miranda, Anthony James. *Youth and Beauty Bright, Coming of Age at Old Boise High, 1901-1921*. Boise: Miranda, 2003.

Neider, Charles. *The Complete Travel Books of Mark Twain, The Early Works: The Innocents Abroad and Roughing It*. Garden City, New York: Doubleday and Co., Inc., 1966.

Neil, J.M. *Discovering Our Surroundings*. Manuscript No. 2/1436. Boise: Idaho State Historical Society Public Archives and Research Library, Ms. 2/1436.

Rising, Marsha Hoffman. *Genealogical Data from the Monmouth Atlas, 1856-1865*. Springfield, Missouri, Hoffman: 1992.

Sermon, Suzanne. "Early Women's Organization in Boise." *Idaho Yesterdays* 41 (Fall 1997): 20-26.

Waite, Thornton. "Boise: On The Main Line at Last." *The Streamliner*, Union Pacific Historical Society. Found at ISHS vertical file, "Boise, Idaho -- Railroad Service and Stations."

Webb, Todd. *The Gold Rush Trail and the Road to Oregon*. Garden City, N.Y.: Doubleday and Co., Inc., 1963.

Wells, Merle W. *Gold Camps and Silver Cities*. Moscow, Idaho: Idaho Department of Lands, Bureau of Mines and Geology, Bulletin 22, 2nd edition, 1983.

World's Columbian Exposition at Chicago, 1893. Published for the Railroad Trade, 1893. No publisher information.

Young, Virgil. *The Story of Idaho*. Moscow: University of Idaho Press, 1977.

Yost, George, and Dick d'Easum. *Idaho: The Fruitful Land*. Boise: Syms-York Company, 1980.

Zhu, Liping. *A Chinaman's Chance*. Boulder: University of Colorado Press, 1997.

WORLD WIDE WEB SITES

"Warren County, IL, History." www.ncig.net/warhist.htm. July 2006.

"Warren County, IL, Resources." www.ncig.net/resources.htm. July 2006.

"Monmouth Atlas." www.mhrising.com/newspapers/monmouth. Click *Monmouth Atlas*. July 19, 2006.

MAPS

Metzger Atlas of Ada County, 1938.

Sanborn Map Company, *Sanborn Fire Insurance Maps for Boise City*, various years. New York: Sanborn Map Company.

MANUSCRIPTS AND MANUSCRIPT COLLECTIONS

Barstow, Elijah Lafayette. ISHS Ms. 2/47. "Copies of letters, 1857-1864."
Coffin, Frank R. IHSH Ms. 521. "Papers of Frank R. Coffin."
Columbian Club of Boise. ISHS Ms. 356. "Records of the Columbian Club."
Neil, J.M. *Discovering Our Surroundings*. ISHS Ms. 2/1436.
Sullivan, Marcella. "An Illustrious Entrepreneur of Idaho." Unpublished manuscript courtesy Linda Leonard Davis.

INTERVIEWS

Marcella Davis Kirby. Interviewed by Patricia Hughes, Caldwell, March 31, 1986.
Davis family descendants. Interviewed by Susan Stacy, Boise, 2006-2007, various dates.

OTHER

Pioneer Cemetery Records, Boise, Idaho.
"Boise, City of Trees: A Centennial History." Idaho Historical Series No. 12. Boise: ISHS, June 1963.
Boise City Archives
Boise High School *Courier* editions.
Idaho State Historical Society Public Archives and Research Library

Index

A

Ada County, 28, 37, 47, 67, 76
Ada County Board of County
    Commissioners, 77, 85
Agnew, James, 29
American Hereford Association, 62
Anderson, George, 88, 89
Apples:
    and labor, 33, 37, 55
    miners' diet, 1, 18, 22, 37, 52
    planting, 1-2, 49-51
    Red June variety, 1-2, 33, 37
    sales, value, marketing, 35, 38, 72,
        78-79, 82
    shipping rates, 68-69
    See also Orchards, Prunes, Peaches.
Army, U.S., 15, 26-28, 61-62
"At-homes," 79
Auburn, Oregon, 18-19

B

Bank Head, Galt, 44
Bank of Commerce, 88
Bannock Street, Boise, 35
Bar O (ranch, brand), 58, 61, 76, 99
Batters, Marion, 44-45
Batters, William, 44-45
Battery Street, Boise, 73
"Binding out." See Indenture.
Bell, Peter, 36
Bible, 4 (illus.), 17
Blackberries, 47, 51
Boise Avenue, Boise, 29
Boise Barracks, 55. *See also* Fort Boise.
Boise Basin:
    Chinese in, 37, 56
    commerce with Boise, 28, 30-31, 34-35
    gold rush, 19-22, 26, 29, 37
    Union convention in, 65

Boise City:
  "building up," x, 48, 65, 69
  as "Eden," 29, 55
  as Idaho Territorial Capitol, 34
  municipal government, 35-37
  and Julia Davis Park, ix, 93-95
  population, 30, 42, 66, 67, 74
  settlement, x, 1, 20, 23-31, 33
  subdividing, 72-74
  town site, founding, 27-29, 33-36, 73
  See also names of streets, parks,
  subdivisions.
Boise City Council, 85, 86, 91
Boise City Hall, 74, 78, 84, 85
Boise City Electric Light Company, 69,
  74
Boise City Original Townsite, 29
Boise foothills, 22, 40, 62-63
Boise High School, 75, 80
Boise Railway and Terminal Company,
  78
Boise Relief Society, 80
Boise River:
  bridges, x, 36, 73
  flooding, spring, 78
  flooding and park site, 86, 93
  and Government Island, 27
  and Oregon Trail, ix, 55
  and railroad grade, 67-69, 78
  and Tom Davis land claim, 22-24, 37
  See also Ditch(es).
Boise Valley:
  attraction for farming, 20, 23, 27
  cattle grazing, 62
  settlement, 20-23, 26-27, 29, 37-8
  traffic to Idaho City, 35
  and Fort Boise, 27
  and Hester Corey Davis, 40
Bollard (Rev.), 52
Brabb, William, 55, 98

Breidensteen, George, 61-62
Bridge, Memorial (Capitol Blvd.), x
Bridge, Ninth Street (Pike), 36, 73
Bristol, Massachusetts, 44
Bristol, Sherlock, 19, 28
Bristow, Elijah, 18, 19
Broad Street, Boise, 72
Bruneau River region, Idaho, 56, 58, 61
Burlend, Rebecca, 6

C

Cabins (Idaho City), 19.
  See also Davis-Ritchey Cabin.
Canal. See Ditch(es).
Canandaigua, New York, 44
Capitol Boulevard, Boise, 72. See also
  Memorial Bridge.
Cartee, Lafayette, 36, 58, 61, 67, 68
Cartee, Mary, 58
Cattle ranching:
  Bar O, 58, 61, 76, 99
  Bruneau, 58-61
  Cascade/Long Valley, 59 (illus.), 62
  Government Island (GI), 58 (illus.),
  61-62, 78, 88
  Herefords, 62
  "cream-colored" (Wm. Batters), 44
  Sparks, John, 52
  Swan Land and Cattle Company, 63
  Texas longhorns, 52
  starving, 18
Census, ix, 11, 12, 37-38, 43
Centerville, 65
Central Pacific Railroad, 37, 49, 66
Central Subdivision, 72
Charleston, 12
Chess club, 43, 94
Chicago, 62, 76, 79, 82, 84

Children:
  of Mary Ann and John Davis, 3-13
  of Tom and Julia Davis, 49-55, 57
      (illus.), 69-71, 74-76, 81, 87-89
  of Henry and Marion McCrum,
      45-48
  poor, 80
  Indian, 24
  See also Davis, Nye, and McCrum
      names; Appendix A.
Chinese:
  gardeners, 62, 92
  labor, 55-56
  miners, 37, 55, 56
Chinese Exclusion Act, 56
Cholera, 6
Cincinnati, Ohio, 3
Civil War, 12-13, 36
Claycomb, Amanda, 11
Claycomb, Andrew, 10 (illus.), 7-15, 22,
  26, 43, 50-51
Claycomb, Harriet Ann Whitman, 4, 8
  (illus.), 7-12, 17, 43
Coffin, Frank, 17, 19, 92
Cold Brook, Warren County, Illinois, 7
Columbian Club of Boise, ix, 76-80,
  83-84, 88, 89, 94
Columbia River, 26
Columbia Theater, Boise, 74, 80, 91
Committee on Flumes and Gulches, 86
Cottonwood Creek, Gulch, Ada
  County, 22, 30
Cottonwood trees, 22, 24
Council Bluffs, Nebraska, 16
County Armaugh, North Ireland, 44
Crane Gulch, Ada County, 51
Crickets, 40
Cutter and Poetz, architects, 77

D

Dairy. See Frank Davis.
Damrosch, Walter, 91, 92
Davis & Himrod store, ix, 58, 59, 60
Davis, Charles A., 42
Davis, Edwin H., 54, 57 (illus.), 93
Davis, Emily, 3, 6
Davis, Francis M. (illus., 25):
  childhood, 3-13
  journey to Boise, 15-19
  marriage, 38, 42
  dairy, 43, 48, 74
  Davis-Ritchey cabin, 23-24
  death, 73-74
  in Idaho City, 19-22
  partnership with Tom Davis, 23-31
  work ethic, 26, 29
  and The Star, 42
  and Boise-Idaho City toll road, 42
Davis, Frank, Addition, 74
Davis, Harry M., 53, 76, 87
Davis, Hazel, 69, 75, 87, 89
Davis, Hester Corey, (illus., 41), 39-43,
  48, 74
Davis, Hester, Addition, 74
Davis, John, 3, 6, 7, 102
Davis, Julia Etta (illus., 57), 53, 57, 75,
  81, 87-89
Davis, Julia McCrum (illus., 90):
  ancestry, 44-47
  Columbian Club member, 76-84
  death, 89
  and death of brother, 61
  geneaology chart, Appendix B
  marriage, 47-48
  and Julia Davis Park, 89-91
  personality, 45-48, 54
  trip to Galt, 49-51
  and World's Fair, 76-84
  See also names of children.

Davis, Marion, 49-52, 75

Davis, Mary Ann, 3, 5-7, 11-12, 16

Davis, Thomas J. (illus., 64):
   childhood, 3-13
   journey to Boise, 15-19, 21 (illus.)
   marriage, 38, 47, 86-87
   as father, 49-52, 75-76, 87-88
   and Hester Corey Davis, 48
   land sales, lease, and development,
      56, 62, 67, 69, 73
   leadership, 65-74
   work ethic, 9-10, 26, 29, 48, 82
   and music, 43, 86, 91-92
   park land gift, 85-87, 89-91, 93-94
   death, 91-92
   See also Apples, Cattle ranching,
      Davis & Himrod store, House,
      Orchards, Railroad.

Davis, Thomas J., Jr., 51, 57 (illus.), 71,
   75-76, 80-83

Davis and McCrum (cattle), 58-61

Davis-Ritchey Cabin, 23-24, 26-29, 38,
   42

Davis & Ritchey's (road house), 30

Davis' (First) Addition, 72, 73

Davis Canyon, Boise County, Idaho, 30

Davis family oral tradition, 12, 48, 86-87

DeLamar, J.R., contest, 80

Denver, Colorado, 82

Depots, Boise, 67-69, 72, 78, 89

Dickson, William, 44

Ditch(es), 22-26, 33, 61-62

Donaldson, Thomas, 43

Dorsey Ferry, 61

Drake, Emma, 53

Dubois, Idaho, 40

DuRell, Benjamin, 29

E

Eastman, Mary, (Mrs. Hosea), 81

"Eden," 29, 55

Eighth Street, Boise, 42, 72, 81, 91

Elk City, Idaho, 17

Elko County, Nevada, 52, 58

Elks (Benevolent Protective Order of),
   89, 92

Ellis, George, 20, 23-24, 33, 37, 43

Elm Grove Park, Boise, 43

Emigrant Road, 54. See also Oregon
   Trail.

Enfield, England, 44

Eoff, Victoria Louise, 77, 80

Episcopal Church, 52, 75

Esquire, 4, 7, 9

Etal, Northumberland, England, 44

F

Fifteen-Mile House, 30

Fifth Street, 72

First Street, Boise, 29

Flanagan, James, 67

Florence, Idaho, 17-18

Foote, Mary Hallock, 77, 79

Fort Boise, 27, 30, 43, 46, 55, 62

Fort Bridger, 16

Fort Hall, Idaho, 16

Fort Lapwai, Idaho, 62

Fort Lemhi, 17

Fort Sumpter, 12, 13

Foundry, Torrance's, 71

Freighting, 26, 29, 30-31, 58, 72

Front Street, Boise, 29, 67, 69, 72, 78

Fruit. See Apples, Peaches, Blackberries.

Fulton Street, Boise, 72, 73

G

Gakey, John and Martha, 73

Gallaudet, J.C. (Rev.), 81

Galt, John, 44

Galt, Ontario, Canada, 44-47, 49, 53, 84, 87-88

Gardeners, Chinese. See Chinese.

Geneaologic chart, Appendix A

General Knox story, 43

GI Ranch. See Government Island.

Gold:

    payment for goods, 1-2, 30-31, 35, 43

    strikes (rush), 15-22, 28, 37

    Tom Davis partners' claim, 26

    value to Union, 26

Government Island, 27, 55, 58 (illus.), 61-62, 73, 88

Government Land Office, 36

Grande River, Oregon, 44

Grand View, Idaho, 61

Grove Street, Boise, 42, 61

H

Hawley, Edgar Thomas, 81

Hawley, James, 28

Heffleman (family), 39, 40

Hereford, 62-63 (illus.)

Heyburn, Ermina, 81

Higgins, C.M., 81

Himrod, Charles, 47, 58, 92

Himrod, Della, 79

Himrod, Hattie, 81

Homestead Act of 1820, 37

Homestead Act of 1862, 19, 23, 37

Hospital, 35, 74

House, Tom and Julia's, 71 (illus.), 72.-74, 89

Huntington, Oregon, 67

Hutton, James, 18

I

Ice skating, 44

Idaho Building, 77, 79, 83

Idaho City:

    Chinese miners, 56

    and traffic with Boise, 26, 27 (illus.), 29-31

    and winter of 1862-63, 19-23

    and James Reynolds, 33-34

    Idaho World, 34

Idaho central mountains, 16-17

Idaho histories, 16, 28

Idaho Statesman (newspaper), quoted or referenced on ix, x, 33-34, 43, 47, 51, 53, 66, 72, 76, 79, 80, 84, 89

Idaho of Yesterday, 43

Idaho State Legislature, 77

Idaho Territory, 3-4, 26, 34, 36, 47

Idaho Street, Boise, 56

Idaho Vitrified Brick and Pipe Company, 88

Idaho World newspaper, 34

Illinois, 1-13, 26, 43, 49, 97

Indenture, 7-9

Indian Creek, Ada County, Idaho, 24, 61, 67

Indians, 17, 23-23

Irrigation. See Ditch(es).

J

Jacobs, Cyrus, 29

Jefferson Street, Boise, 77

John Davis, 5

Johnson, Sarah, 11

Julia Davis Park, Boise, x, 85-86, 89-91, 93-95 (illus.), Appendix B

K

Kelly, Milton, 34, 52
Kelton, Utah, 49, 58, 66
Kentucky, 4, 7, 9
Keokuk, Iowa, 16
Krall, John, 68, 69
Kuna, Idaho, 67, 73

L

Labor:
    at Davis orchard, 31, 37, 54-56
    and Julia McCrum Davis, 47, 54-56
    general need for, 30, 40, 62
Lake Michigan, 79
Land Office, 37
Land sales:
    real estate as business, 34
    Tom Davis', 8, 35, 67, 69, 71, 73
Lemhi Valley, 16
Lewiston, Idaho, 34
Library, Boise, 84, 85
Lincoln, Abraham, 12-13, 19, 26
Littel, Dave, 23, 24
Long Valley, Idaho, 62-63
Lugenbeel, Pinkney, Maj., 26-30

M

Main Street, Boise, 28-29, 33, 35, 42, 58, 71
Masonic Cemetery, 52, 89, 92
McClellan, John, 24, 29
McConnell, William J., Governor, 81
McCrum & Deary store, 53
McCrum, Charles, 53
McCrum, Henry (grandfather of Julia), 44-45
McCrum, Henry (father of Julia), 44, 45 (illus.), 46

McCrum, Jessie, 53
McCrum, Marion Batters, 45-46 (illus.), 47, 53
McCrum, John Edwin, 53, 76, 87-89, 93
McCrum, Richard, 45
McCrum, LaVerne, 89
McKay, Donald ("Cap"), 20, 23
McPherson, Alex, 71-72
McRay's Gap, Boise County, 30
Memorial Bridge, Boise, x, 72
Methodist (church), 73
Miller (family), 42
Miller, John, 11
Miners' cabin (Idaho Building), 77, 83
Mining and miners:
    Auburn, 18-19
    Florence, 17-18
    Boise Basin, 19-24, 26
    Nevada, 52
    hospital, 35
    appeal to McCrum brothers, 46
    See also Chinese.
Mississippi River, 3, 16
Monday Afternoon Club, 88, 89
Monmouth, Illinois, 3-7, 11-13, 15-16
Monmouth Atlas, 9, 12, 13, 16
Montana, 40, 43
Moore's Creek, Boise County, 30
Mormon story, 16-17
Music, 43, 53, 77-81, 91
Music box, 86 (illus.), 87
Music Committee (of Columbian Club), 91-92
Myrtle Street, Boise, 72

N

Nampa, Idaho, 67, 69
Natatorium, 77-78
Native Americans, 38. See also Indians.

Nebraska, 15, 16
Nevada, 43, 52, 58, 63
Newton (Rev.), 42
New York City, 89
New York Philharmonic Orchestra, 91
Ninth Street, 35, 67, 72, 73, 91
Ninth Street Bridge, 36
Ninth Street Pike, 73
North End, Boise, 43
Nye, "baby," 51, 52
Nye's drug store, 53
Nye House, 42

O

O'Farrell, John A., 35
Oberlin, Ohio, 76
Olmstead, Henry Law, 82
Omaha, Nebraska, 39
Opal, Idaho, 80
Oquawka, Illinois, 16
Oral tradition. See Davis family oral
    tradition.
Orchards:
    Crange Gulch, 51
    description, ix, 47
    of Frank Davis, 43
    and labor, 33, 37, 55
    management, 37, 43, 47, 48-49
    marketing, 22, 37, 43, 51-52, 72
    planting, 1-2, 33, 49-50
    removal of, 73-74
    See also Apples, Prunes, Peaches.
Oregon Short Line (OSL) Railroad, 61,
    62, 66-69, 72, 82
Oregon Trail, ix, x, 26, 29-42. See also
    Platte River Road; Emigrant Road;
    Davis, Hester Corey; Davis, Thomas
    J.; Main Street.

Orofino, Idaho, 16
Ostner, Charles, 65
Overland House, 42, 43
Owyhee County, 43, 58

P

Palmer, Bertha, 76
Panic of 1893, 82
Parks, 85-86, 117, Appendix B.
Payette, Idaho, 19, 62
Peaches, 43, 47, 79
Peoria, Illinois, 4, 13
Perrault, Delphine, 52
Philharmonic Orchestra, New York, 81
Philips Exeter Academy, New
    Hampshire, 76
Pickel, Hugh, 42, 48
Pierce, Idaho, 16
Pinney, James (Mayor), 81, 85
Pinney Theater, 91
Pioneer Cemetery. See Masonic
    Cemetery.
Pioneering:
    in Canada, 44-45
    in Illinois, 3-13
    in Idaho, x, 4, 23-31
    Pioneer Village, x, Appendix B.
Placerville, Idaho, 23
Platte River Road, 15-16, 39
Pleasanton Addition, 74
Pony Express, 15
Population:
    Warren County, 4, 9
    Boise Basin, 22
    Elko area, Nevada, 52
    Chinese, 56
    Boise, 74
Portland, Oregon, 1, 26, 29, 66-67

Prairie Farmer (magazine), 9
Prickett, Henry, Mayor, 36
Prunes, 72
Purdom tract, 62

Q

Quinn, William, 89

R

Railroad:
    Main line to Boise, 66-69, 72, 78, 82
    Boise depot, 67, 69, 72, 78, 82
    and Tom Davis, 63, 65-74
    rates, 68-69, 79, 91
Railroad(s). See Boise Railway and
    Terminal Company, Central Pacific,
    Oregon Short Line (OSL), Union
    Pacific Railroad, Utah and Northern.
Red June apples, 2, 33
Regan, Rose, (Mrs. Timothy), 81
Republican Party, 12. *See also* Union.
Reynolds, James, 33, 34, 39, 40
Richardson, Mrs., 88
Riggs, Henry C., 29, 34
Ritchey, William L., 19-24, 27-28, 33-35,
    37, 43. *See also* Davis-Ritchey Cabin.
Riverside Pavilion, Boise, 91
Robie Creek, Boise County, 30
Roseola, 52
Round Valley, Idaho, 62

S

Salt Lake City, 15
Sanborn map, 70 (illus.)
Sawmill, 27, 30
School tax election, 66, 94
Scotland, 44

Scurvy, 18
Seventh Street, Boise, 42, 72
Shade, Absolom, 44
Shade's Mills, 44
Shaw Mountain, 30
Sheep, 61, 74
Shipping rates, fruit, 68-69
Shoshoni Indians, 23
Shoup, George L., Senator, 83
Six Nations, 44
Sixteenth Street, Boise, 29
Skovil, Polaski, 5-6
Slater, Thomas, 1, 24
Slavery, 12
Smith (Doctor), 61
Smith, Peter, 39
Snake River, 48, 56, 79
Social gatherings, 79, 80
South Carolina, 12
Southern Nez Perce Trail, 17
South Pass, Wyoming, 16, 17
Sparks, John, 52, 63
St. Joseph, Missouri, 16
St. Margaret's Academy, 75
St. Michael's Episcopal Church, 75
Stagecoach, 27 (illus.)
Standifer, Jeff, 24
Star, the, roadhouse, 30-31, 42-43
State Street, Boise, 48
Steamboat Springs, Boise Basin, 20
Stevens, (Doctor), 52
Steward, Mrs. George H., 78
Stewart (family), 40, 42
Stilts, G.W., 35
Straughn, Alice, 76-77, 79
Streets, Boise. See street names.
"Stub," the, 69
Subdividing, 72-74
Sublette's Cutoff, 16

Subscribing, 65-66, 67, 69, 85, 94
Swan Land and Cattle Company, 63

T

Table Rock, Ada County, 30
Telephone, 43, 85
Tenth Street, Boise, 42, 69
Territorial Capitol, 34
Territorial legislature, 26, 30, 35, 36, 65, 71
Thibado, Dr. Augustus, 47
Thibado, Mary, 46
Thirteenth Street, Boise, 88
Thompson, W.L., 24
Toll road, Boise to Idaho City, 30, 35
Torrance, Marcella, 89
Torrance foundry, 71
Town and Village Improvement (Columbian Club), 84, 86
Townsite (Auburn), 18-19
Townsite (Boise). See Boise City.
Transcontinental railroad, 37.
    See also Central Pacific Railroad.
Twain, Mark, 15
Twelfth Street, Boise, 67
Twenty-first Street, Boise, 48

U

Umatilla, 1, 2, 26
Union, federal, 26, 65
Union Pacific Railroad, 62, 66-68, 78
University of Notre Dame, Indiana, 76, 87
Utah and Northern Railroad, 66-67

V

Van Wyck, Valley County, Idaho, 62

W

Walla Walla, Washington, 18
Warm Springs, the, Boise, 23-24
Warren County, Illinois, 3-13
Washington, George, statue, 65-66, 68 (illus.)
Water Street, Boise, 73
Wells, James M., 79
"White City," 82
"Wild west," 47
Willey, Norman, Gov., 76
Women:
    partners of Frank and Tom Davis, 39-48,
    social gatherings, 53, 79-80, 88
    Brabb sisters, 55
    See also Columbian Club.
Women's Board of Lady Managers (World's Fair), 76
Women's Building, 82 (illus.), 84
Women's Congress, 83
Women's Reception Room, 77
Women's Sphere, 84
Wood River, Idaho mining area, 43
World's Fair. See World's Columbian Exposition.
World's Columbian Exposition, 76-84

About T&J Publishing...

T&J Publishing is a non-profit company created by Diane Davis Mykelgard of Boise, great-granddaughter of Tom and Julia Davis of Boise, and daughter of Tom and Jemima Davis of Cascade. The company publishes historical works about Idaho subjects.

Tom and Julia Davis: "Some Good Place," Boise, Idaho $19.95
By Susan M. Stacy   ISBN 978-0-9798767-1-4

Tom Davis left Illinois in 1861, headed for the mining frontier of the Far West. Surviving an unusually harrowing journey across Idaho's central mountains, he found himself rejecting El Dorado in favor of an apple orchard on the banks of the Boise River.

Tom found his life partner when Julia McCrum left her parents' home in Galt, Canada, for her own adventure in the West, demonstrating that the "Wander Lust" could infect women just as readily as men.

Tom and Julia Davis: Some Good Place tells what happened next — the creation of a city sometimes called an "Eden," business successes, the joys and tragedies of family life. This remarkable couple gave Boise City the land for Julia Davis Park. What were they thinking? Author Susan Stacy has a pretty good idea, and tells the story with compelling detail, sympathy, and insight.

The Resurrection of the Bar O $24.95
By Tom and Jemima Davis   ISBN 978-0-9798767-0-7

Forsaking opulent turn-of-the-19th-century Boise for grassy pastures in south-central Idaho and eastern Oregon, the Davis family embarked on the demanding life of 20th-century ranching and never looked back. Here, in their own words, they travel old trails again, from cattle drives to meetings where million-dollar
deals were sealed with a handshake and a glass of Scotch. In a 60- year period, Tom Davis bought and sold 22 ranches — a feat impossible in the 21st century. This book tells how he did it.

Woven throughout are Jemima Davis' recollections and recipes, anecdotes from friends, family, and business associates, and photos of ranch life from the 1800s to today at Emmett, near Cascade, Jordan Valley, Vale, and the historic Alvord below Steens Mountain.

The Resurrection of the Bar O, richly illustrated, is a coming-of-age saga of the American West and the pioneers who built it.

To order: T&J Publishing
         3100 Crescent Rim Drive, Suite 408
         Boise, Idaho 83706
         (208) 344-9929

T&J PUBLISHING
Boise, Idaho